The Story
of India

Childcraft

The Story of India – a **Childcraft** title
2nd printing 1991
Childcraft Reg. US Pat. Off. Marca Registrada

Copyright © 1990 by World Book, Inc.
525 West Monroe Street
Chicago, Illinois 60661
USA

Printed in the USA

ISBN 0-7166-6497-6

B/IA

The Story of India

World Book International
a World Book Company
Chicago London Sydney

Publishing Director: Felicia Bailey
Managing Editor: Pip Morgan
Project Editor: Gerry Bailey
Editor: Alice Webb
Authors: Gerry Bailey
                       Andrew Langley

Design and
    Pre-press Manager: Christine McKenzie
Designer: Frank Peglar
Picture Research: Samantha Bentham

Consultants: Sadashiv V. Gorakshkar
                       Director, Prince of Wales Museum of
                       Western India, Bombay

                       Anjuli Kaul MA
                       History Specialist, Bombay International
                       School, Bombay

                       Prof. A. K. Jalaluddin
                       UNICEF Consultant and formerly, Director,
                       National Council of Educational Research
                       and Training, New Delhi — team leader

                       Prof. Arjun Dev
                       Head, Department of Education in
                       Social Science and Humanities, NCERT,
                       New Delhi

                       Mr Santo Datta
                       Editor, Publication Department, NCERT,
                       New Delhi

                       Mr K. Ramachandran
                       Reader, Department of Pre-School and
                       Elementary Education, NCERT, New Delhi

Contents

The first Indians

In the still jungle, a band of dark-skinned hunters crouched. They could hear something making its way through the trees and bushes. Slowly, they raised their weapons.

Suddenly, a frightened deer charged out of the bushes towards them. The hunters leaped to their feet and hurled their long spears at it. Within seconds, the wounded deer had fallen to the ground. It had been a good day's work! The hunters hung the deer from a pole to carry it back to the camp. It would make a delicious meal when cooked with the herbs and roots gathered in the jungle during the day.

These people probably lived in India as long ago as 100,000 BC. We call them Paleolithic, or Old Stone Age, people because they made tools out of stone. Little is known about them. Among the earliest Indian people about whom we know something, were the Negroids. There were also groups we call Proto-Australoids, who looked similar to the native peoples of Australia, Mongoloids from the north-east, and Mediterraneans.

After about 10,000 BC, these hunters and gatherers learned how to tame wild animals and how to plant crops, such as wheat and barley. This was an important development. Now each tribe, or group, could settle down in one place without having to move frequently in search of food. We call these the Neolithic, or New Stone Age, people. They could build villages out of mud brick huts, look after their cattle, and even paint beautiful pottery.

This change in the way the Indian people lived took a long time to happen and is called the Neolithic, or agricultural, revolution.

The Harappans

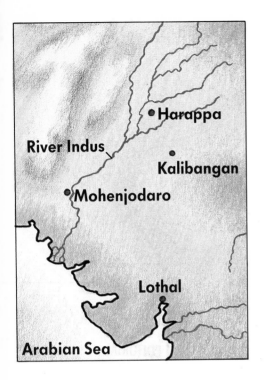

This map shows where the Harappan civilization developed.

The wealthy farmer watched as the last cart-load of wheat pulled up at the threshing yard. He was pleased! Once again, his storehouse was almost filled to the top with grain. He would do good business when the Sumerian traders arrived to buy.

The farmer lived almost four thousand years ago on land which bordered the great Indus River and its tributaries. He was part of what we now call the Harappan civilization. By 2300 BC, the people of this civilization had formed an organized society and had built cities. The magnificent walled city of Harappa gives the civilization its name.

Harappa thrived for over five hundred years, and was probably the northern 'capital' of the civilization. Mohenjodaro was the southern capital and another important city. Today, archaeologists have found remains of over a hundred towns and cities built on or around the great plain of the Indus valley.

We can learn much about the culture of this civilization from sites such as Lothal in Gujarat and Kalibangan in Rajasthan. This culture once stretched for about 1,000 kilometres from east to west, and 1,100 kilometres from north to south, and was the largest in the world.

Outside the cities, the Indus people grew crops such as wheat and barley. Their farms did well because they had discovered how to bring water to, or irrigate, their fields. They stored any grain they didn't use in huge storehouses, or granaries, or they traded it for the other products they needed.

As well as growing crops, the farmers kept
domestic animals, such as poultry, goats,
sheep, cattle and dogs. The Indus people were
among the first in the world to make carts
which had wheels.

Inside the cities, skilled workers, or artisans,
made ornaments out of copper, bronze, silver
and gold which were often decorated with
precious stones. Other craftsmen made tools,
such as knives, sickles and fish-hooks. Potters
designed red pots decorated with black, and
weavers made cloth out of cotton.

The great bath

The architect watched proudly as the great bath slowly filled with water. It had taken many months of hard work to complete, but now the buildings and the bath itself looked splendid! The ceremonies that would be performed here would surely be very successful!

The architect didn't realize just how long his building would last. Before 1925, nobody realized that it even existed. But then the bath was discovered by archaeologists among the ancient ruins of the city of Mohenjodaro.

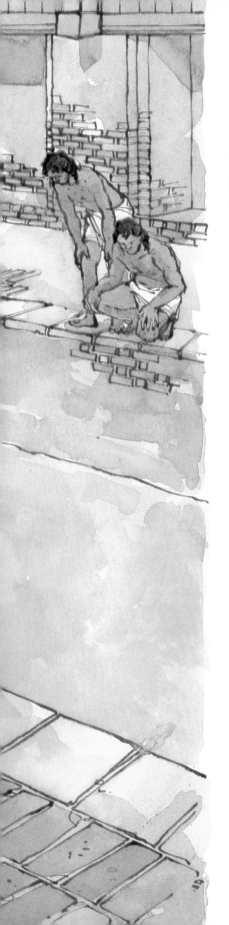

The Harappans must have lived very ordered and civilized lives. We know this from the way in which their cities and buildings were planned.

Mohenjodaro was one of the two most important cities of the Harappan people. It was built out of 'burned' bricks and surrounded by a high wall which protected the people inside from enemies and floods. The streets were very straight and the houses were often shaped like a rectangle, with an open space, or courtyard, in the middle. House and street wells provided drinking water, and covered drains drew the street sewage away from people's houses and then out of the city.

The city was divided into two parts, an inner area, or citadel, and the 'lower town'. In the citadel stood temples, granaries and an assembly hall, as well as the great bath. The lower town was where most of the people actually lived.

The quality of the bricks used to build these cities was so good that they were used to build a railway line in the 19th century.

The Harappan civilization lasted for over five hundred years. Then something terrible happened which destroyed it. We don't know what this was. Some historians believe that the Harappan people were massacred by invaders from the north. Others believe that floods were to blame. Whatever the disaster, it marked the end of one of the greatest civilizations of the ancient world.

The coming of the Aryans

As the light chariot thundered away, pulled by two horses, the charioteer stood up. He held a shield in one hand and a spear in the other. He called out to his men who thrust their weapons into the air with a tremendous shout of support.

These were the Aryans. They were skilful fighters who came from the cold, grassy plains of Central Asia, north-west of the Hindu Kush mountains, and travelled south into the Indus valley. Here, they probably defeated the last of the Harappan people. The galloping horses must have been a terrifying sight to the earlier inhabitants of northern India, who had probably never seen such animals before.

Slowly, over the centuries, these bold warriors and adventurers moved eastwards until they had settled in the plain of the Ganga. Here, they drove out the original inhabitants whom they called the 'dasyus'.

The Aryans were nomads, which means they moved from place to place. They formed small family groups known as tribes, which were ruled by a chief, and they kept herds of cattle, goats, sheep and horses. The most important of these animals were the cattle. A man was rich if he owned a lot of cows.

As these tribes spread eastwards and became more settled, their villages grew. Cities like Hastinapur were founded. The Aryans began to plant crops, such as wheat, barley and cotton.

The Aryans came to be divided into four groups, or 'classes'. These classes were called 'varnas'.

The highest class was that of the priests, or 'brahmins'. Next came the warriors, or 'kshatriyas', followed by the peasant farmers, artisans and traders. These were the 'vaishyas'. The lowest class was that of the menial servants and labourers, or 'shudras'.

This system of dividing people into classes according to what they did became known as the 'caste' system.

Words of wisdom

Dawn broke slowly. A group of young men were listening, spellbound, to an old priest with a long white beard. He was squatting in front of them, singing a beautiful hymn in the Sanskrit language.

'The daughter of Heaven has appeared with the light:
Young woman in flaming garb
Who reigns on all the earth.
Blessed dawn, shine on us today.'

This verse comes from a collection of hymns called the 'Rig Veda'. Young priests, or brahmins, from north-west India would have chanted it in Sanskrit over three thousand years ago. It was composed by Aryan people sometime between 1500 BC and 1000 BC. The Aryans loved literature and music, and we can find out quite a lot about them from the words of the Vedic hymns.

As there was no script in which they could write down the Vedas, brahmins developed amazing memories. They could recite line after line without making a single mistake. They learned to recite them forwards, backwards and in different patterns. Any mistake could be spotted at once.

We say that these works were composed by Aryan people, but we mustn't forget that Aryans had been mixing with the earlier inhabitants of the country. So the culture that developed during this period was really the work of a mixture of people.

Indra and Vritra

Once, there were no rain clouds and there was no rain. The Earth was in a pitiful state. The land had become dry and shrunken under the parching and relentless heat of the Sun.

The wicked demon of drought and famine was called Vritra. Vritra lived high up in the atmosphere in huge towers made of clouds. He was the enemy of Indra, who was the lord of all the gods.

Many of the hymns, or poems, of the Vedas were sung to Indra. He was powerful and noble. He was the son of Heaven and Earth, the warrior god and the god of crashing thunder and drenching rain.

During the drought, the people prayed for a saviour to bring them rain. In answer to their prayers, Indra, the lord of the gods, reached into the atmosphere and grabbed a vajra, a shining thunderbolt, to use as a weapon. Then he seized a rainbow to use as a bow. Greedily, he drank huge gulps of soma juice, the energy-giving drink of the gods. With each gulp, he grew braver and more confident.

At last, Indra was ready to meet his enemy, Vritra. Indra could change into many different forms, so he was able to attack Vritra again and again, until the god of drought could no longer defend himself. Eventually, Vritra was thrown out from his cloudy towers.

The people were overjoyed at Indra's victory, and the rains fell once again on the Earth. But it wasn't the end of Vritra. He was drought, and drought can never be banished from the world for ever.

Vritra would lie in wait. He would watch and make wicked plans. Then one day, he would return to parch the Earth once more.

Ashvatthama's death

The 'Mahabharata' and the 'Ramayana' are great epic poems, full of action, colour and excitement. They tell us many things about the people who lived in northern India more than two thousand years ago.

One of the stories from the 'Mahabharata' goes like this. Long, long ago, there lived two families descended from two brothers. They were called the Kauravas and the Pandavas.

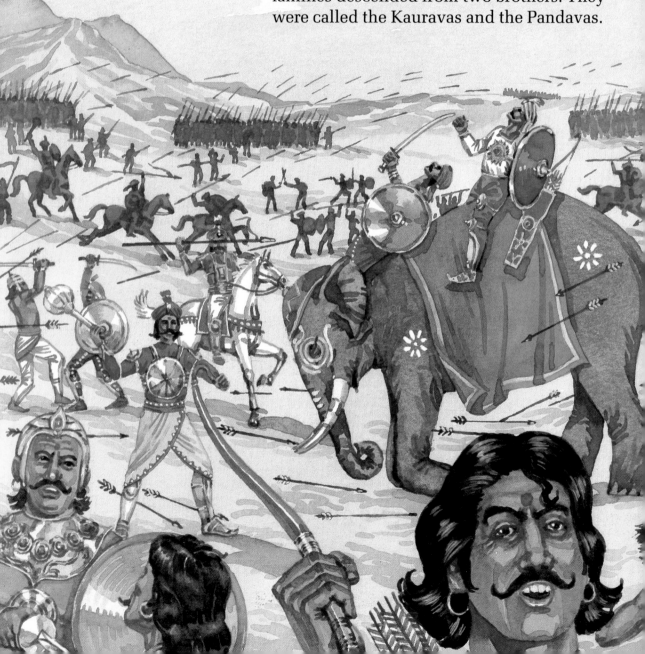

Both families of cousins thought that they had the right to rule the Kingdom of Hastinapur. The Kauravas were evil men. They managed to drive the good Pandavas out of the kingdom and refused to share their land. This quarrel grew and grew until at last the families went to war against each other.

The Pandavas fought bravely, but they couldn't hope to win while the great warrior, Drona, commanded the enemy troops. But on the fifteenth day of the war, the Pandavas had some good fortune. An elephant, called Ashvatthama, was killed. As it happened, Drona's son was also called Ashvatthama! So the clever Pandavas spread the rumour that Ashvatthama was dead.

When Drona heard this rumour, he was naturally very upset. Had his son really been killed? In order to find out the truth, Drona summoned Yudhishthira, the eldest of the Pandava brothers, to come before him. Yudhishthira couldn't tell lies. He couldn't even tell lies to an enemy.

But Yudhishthira was a clever man. He told Drona, "Yes, the elephant Ashvatthama is dead". But he spoke the words "the elephant" so softly that Drona couldn't hear them. Drona was so shocked at the news that he fell into a trance, and almost at once, a Pandava warrior cut off his head.

Drona's death weakened the Kauravas, and eventually, they lost the war. At last, the Pandavas were able to rule the Kingdom of Hastinapur.

The Buddha

Over two and a half thousand years ago, there ruled a King of the Sakya tribe. The king didn't want his son the prince to give up the pleasures of the world to become a hermit, so he surrounded him with all the wonders of palace life. He especially made sure that whenever the prince left the palace, he saw no sign of suffering or sorrow.

But the prince, Siddhartha, soon grew curious. He wanted to see what lay beyond this life of luxury. One night, he rode out into the town with his charioteer.

There, Siddhartha saw the old and the sick and dead. He was dismayed. He began to think deeply about the cause of such misery. How could it be prevented? Siddhartha knew that he must give up everything to find out. So one day, he left his wife and son, and began to wander the land with only a begging bowl.

Siddhartha started his search by talking to wise priests. But the priests lived lives of ease, comfort and wealth. None of them could help him. Then one evening, as Siddhartha was sitting deep in thought under a large tree, he suddenly knew that he had found the truth.

Siddhartha decided that people should live simple lives. They shouldn't hurt or kill people or animals. The 'caste' system of dividing people up into groups, or classes, should be abandoned. From that moment, Siddhartha became known as the 'Enlightened One', or the 'Buddha'.

When the Buddha died at the age of eighty, he had gathered many followers about him. Today, his teachings are followed by millions of people all over the world.

Takshashila

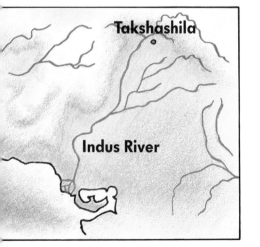

The city of Takshashila lies in north-west India.

While the Buddha was alive, many of the towns in India were quite small. But as time passed, great cities grew up, like Shravasti, Rajagriha, Kashi and Takshashila.

In about 550 BC, the north-western city of Takshashila was a great centre for trade and learning. Clever young men were often sent there to complete their education. They came from Magadha, the most important kingdom in northern India.

In Takshashila, these young men learnt from a guru, or teacher. Each guru taught religion and philosopy, and also a special subject, like mathematics, medicine or astronomy.

Panini, a scholar from Takshashila during the 4th century BC, was one of the most learned men of his time. He became famous for his grammar of the Sanskrit language.

The city of Takshashila was built on a grid system, much like the earlier cities of Mohenjodaro and Harappa. Its main street ran from north to south and was about six metres wide. From this street, smaller ones branched off at right angles. The city was well planned and well organized.

The ruins of the city have now been excavated, or uncovered. They show that three cities, Bhir Mound, Sirkap and Sirsukh, have been built here at different times.

These marks were punched onto silver coins used at Magadha.

Alexander and Porus

King Porus shouted out the order to charge. The chariots of his huge army surged forward through a sea of mud and stones. Ahead, waited the soldiers of Alexander, King of Macedon. He had crossed the Jhelum River that night to attack Porus's troops.

Alexander was the most brilliant commander of his time. He had led his troops out of Macedonia, in Greece, to conquer as much of the world as he could. So far, his soldiers had been victorious.

Now, Alexander had come into north-west India to raid King Porus's territory, and to defeat his army beside the Jhelum River.

Alexander's cavalry waited for the right moment, then they charged Porus's oncoming troops. Within minutes, the Macedonians had taken charge of the battle. Desperate fighting continued all day, until most of Porus's soldiers had been slaughtered. In the end, King Porus was forced to surrender.

Porus was wounded in nine places on his body, but he faced Alexander with dignity. When he was asked how he wished to be treated, he replied boldly, "As a king!" Alexander felt great respect for such a brave man. He decided to allow Porus to continue ruling his territory.

After Alexander had won the battle, he began to move farther east. But his army was tired and homesick after years of marching and fighting. His soldiers refused to continue, and Alexander decided to return home.

On the journey back to Greece, Alexander's soldiers faced many hardships. Half of them died from fighting or through sickness. And when their journey took them along the coast of Iran and into Babylon, Alexander himself died, either of malaria, or perhaps of alcohol poisoning.

Alexander drove his army north-west into India. Before going home, he divided his army into three groups under different leaders. Each group returned along a separate route.

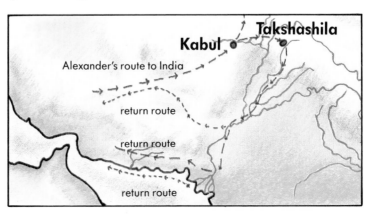

Chandragupta's rule

Chandragupta watched as the little boy put down his dish. The boy's mother was scolding him. "Don't eat from the centre of the dish," she warned. "It's far too hot – you'll burn your mouth! Eat from the sides of the dish, where the food's cooler."

Chandragupta Maurya smiled to himself. Then he became serious, and began to think about the woman's words. "That's it!" he thought. "Now I know how to defeat Magadha. I shall attack from the edge of the kingdom first, then move slowly in towards the capital of Pataliputra."

Magadha was the strongest kingdom in India and had had many rulers. Chandragupta became the most powerful ruler of them all. First, he gathered together an army, then he forced the last of the Nanda rulers off the throne. Then, in about 321 BC, Chandragupta became king. During his reign, the capital, Pataliputra, was one of the greatest cities in the world.

Chandragupta set about gaining more territory. Eventually, he made his empire so large that it spread across nearly the whole of the subcontinent of India.

Chandragupta didn't become powerful all by himself. It is likely that a wise old brahmin, called Kautilya, became his chief minister. Kautilya had helped him come to power. He wrote a book on how to govern, and talked to Chandragupta about governing a country, organizing money and behaving as a king. Kautilya also helped Chandragupta to form the laws in Magadha.

Chandragupta was only really challenged once. This was by the powerful Greek king, Seleucus. Seleucus wanted to capture the Punjab, but Chandragupta defeated him. After that, the two men became friends. In 297 BC, Chandragupta gave up his throne to his son, Bindusara, then fasted until he died.

Emperor Ashoka

Ashoka built tall pillars, like this one, on which the words of his edicts were carved.

The minister walked slowly up to the Emperor Ashoka. He bowed, then handed the emperor a pile of palm-leaf papers. On these papers were written the accounts of the minister's department. If the clerks had done their job well, the figures would be correct and the emperor would be pleased.

When Ashoka became the leader of the Mauryan Empire in 273 BC, almost all of India was under his rule. The only areas he didn't control were some lands at the southern tip of the sub-continent, and the Kingdom of Kalinga. Ashoka decided to use his great power to crush Kalinga.

During the war which followed, thousands of men were killed and wounded, and thousands more driven from their homes. When the war ended, Ashoka decided that he didn't want to fight any more. He was possibly the first ruler in history to give up war as a means of getting what he wanted.

Within a few years, Ashoka had become a follower of the Buddhist religion. He began to see himself as the father of his people. He made special edicts, or proclamations, about being tolerant, not fighting, and looking after others. These were a kind of code of conduct for his people. The language of the edicts wasn't Sanskrit, but Prakrit, the language of the common people. The words were carved in a script called 'Brahmi'. It is the first known system of writing to come down to us since Harappan times.

The words of the edicts were carved into huge pillars and rocks so that everyone could read them. Government workers made sure that everyone lived and worked according to these edicts. The pillars were erected all over the kingdom, and many of them can still be seen today.

The Great Stupa

The Emperor Ashoka was worried. He wanted to express his devotion to the Buddha, but he wasn't sure how to do it. After thinking long and hard, he decided to build brick mounds called 'stupas' in the Buddha's honour.

Stupas stand in many places throughout India, and in some parts of Asia. They are all dedicated to the Buddha and his relics are placed in them. The first stupas were simple, dome-shaped buildings. Those built later were taller and more magnificent. Often, it is possible to tell in which region a stupa was built by its style and design.

One of the most famous stupas is the Great Stupa at Sanchi. It was begun by Emperor Ashoka and made larger and more beautiful after his death. Ashoka's builders probably only finished the inner brick core. Wooden gates and railings may have been placed around it afterwards. In about 100 BC, the wooden parts were replaced by wonderful carved stones. The Sanchi Stupa is one of the earliest surviving works of Buddhist architecture.

This is the north gate of the Great Stupa at Sanchi. This section of the railing shows the intricate carving. It is made of red sandstone.

The caves at Ajanta were hidden for hundreds of years. They were rediscovered in 1819.

The Ajanta caves

The members of the hunting party could hardly believe their eyes! Before them stood a row of magnificent caves carved into the side of the rocky gorge, on a bend of the Waghora River.

The year was 1819. A British hunting party had discovered the Ajanta caves, a wonderful collection of ancient Buddhist temples and monasteries. The caves were so well hidden that they had stood there for hundreds of years, and no one had known they were there.

The Buddhist monks who carved the temples and monasteries probably began work on them in about 200 BC. They had carved out rooms and chambers where they could live and pray.

The monks continued this work until about AD 650. They were provided for by several of the ruling families of India.

The monks were very skilful. They carved the rock and then decorated it with large murals, or wall-paintings. These paintings are rich and colourful and full of life. They tell stories of the Buddha, and show how people should behave and treat each other.

The paintings may have been started before the Christian era. They show kings and court life, as well as the lives of ordinary men and women, and musicians and animal life. They help us understand how people lived during that time.

Visitors from all over the world have admired the style of these cave paintings. It is easy to see how they have influenced modern painters today.

Generations of monks created the wall-paintings of Ajanta.

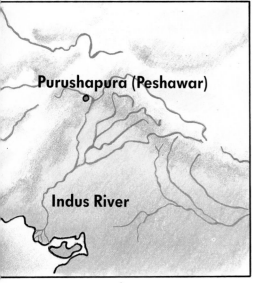

Purushapura (Peshawar)

Indus River

The Kushan Empire lay in the north-west of India.

The Kushan Empire

The travellers shielded their eyes as they urged their horses into the icy wind that swirled around them. They wore heavy coats and padded boots to help keep out the cold. But still it crept in. Each man knew that the crossing over the high mountain passes into northern India was going to be hard and very dangerous.

The travellers were bound for the city of Purushapura, which today is called Peshawar. It lay at the centre of the great trade routes that ran from China and India to the West.

Here, the travellers would be able to trade for goods from all over India, and perhaps from China as well. With luck, they could become wealthy men.

Purushapura was the capital city of the third Kushan emperor, Kanishka. The Kushan people had come from Central Asia, driven out of their homelands by other tribes. Around AD 50, they moved west and south into north-west India, where they soon defeated the tribes they met, and quickly took control.

The first Kushan king to rule in northern India was called Kujula Kadphises. When he died, after eighty years of rule, he left his empire to his son, Vima. Vima liked the Indian way of life. He issued gold coins, copying the Indian ones, not the Roman type of coins his father had minted.

The next emperor, Kanishka, was a Buddhist and the greatest of the Kushan leaders. His wealth and wisdom attracted poets, artists, musicians and monks to Purushapura from all over Asia. Schools of art flourished at Mathura and Gandhara. The successful empire encouraged trade, and merchants made journeys from distant lands to trade in the Kushan capital.

Kanishka is thought to have started a new era which we call the 'Shaka' era. It began in AD 78. This is now used as the official calendar of India, along with the standard, or Gregorian, calendar.

This Kushan coin and statue show the figure of Kanishka.

Healing with herbs

The student stepped forward enthusiastically and handed the plant to his master, Charaka. Charaka took the plant, looking at it carefully. It was a very good specimen! Then he turned to a large, well-thumbed book, and began leafing through the pages. The student watched with concentration.

Suddenly, Charaka stopped and pointed to a page. There was a picture of the plant, along with a description of it and an account of the ways in which it could be used to make medicines. The student smiled happily.

This book is known today as the 'Charaka Samhita'. It is the oldest medical textbook to have survived in India, and was partly written by Charaka during the reign of the Emperor Kanishka.

A great deal of work was done by Indians in ancient times in the field of healing and medicine. They paid special attention to medicines made from herbs. In one of the Vedas, there are recipes for potions to help people live longer.

The 'Charaka Samhita' has eight sections and is divided into a hundred and fifty chapters. It mentions over six hundred drugs that come from animals, plants and minerals.

The book also instructs the people of the medical profession on how to behave. A doctor 'must not betray his patients, even at the cost of his own life.' Most doctors today have to take an oath very similar to this one, before they can practise medicine.

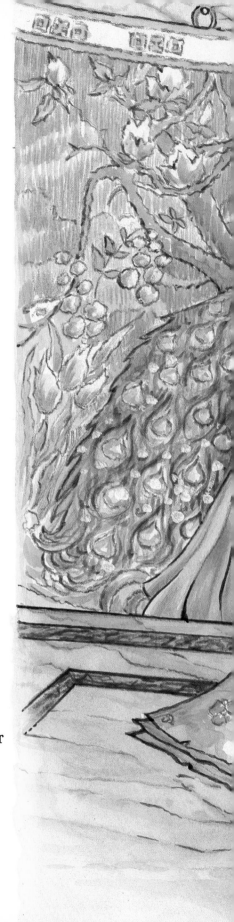

A poets' gathering

'The farmers who harvest rice in the hot sun now leap into the waves of the clear sea. The sailors, captains of stout craft, drink strong liquor and dance for joy, as they clasp the bright-bangled hands of women who wear garlands of clustering punnai.'

This beautiful verse describes the life of ordinary people, and is taken from a poem written about two thousand years ago. The poem was part of a large collection of poems called the 'Eight Anthologies' written in the ancient Tamil language. Unlike modern Tamil, this language has to be studied very carefully before it can be read and properly understood.

The collection contains over two thousand poems written by more than two hundred poets. It includes love poems, poems that praise heroes and kings, poems written to the gods, and poems that rejoice in festivals and people having fun.

No one knows exactly when the 'Eight Anthologies' was written. A Tamil legend tells of three great meetings of writers and poets held in the ancient town of Madurai, called 'Sangams'. These were wonderful festivals of poetry and music.

The poets of the Tamil region would probably have wandered through the countryside, reciting their poems to kings and villagers alike. Then, at the time of the Sangam, they would have gathered at Madurai. Many poems were composed at these gatherings, including the 'Eight Anthologies', ten long poems, and a work on Tamil grammar called the 'Tolkappiyam'.

The 'Eight Anthologies' is one of the greatest works of Tamil literature.

Wonderful zero

A boy was crouching in the courtyard under a shady tree. In the dust, he was scratching out the symbols from one to nine. Then he thoughtfully drew the symbol for 'one' followed by the symbol for 'zero'. In his head, he knew that he had made ten.

The decimal place system had nine digits and a zero, which meant that new numbers could be formed. Today, this seems a simple and obvious idea, but in the 6th century it was new. Up until then, no one had been able to use zero in mathematics or to write numbers as we do. In India, Greece and other countries, numbers were written with separate symbols for tens and hundreds. In the Roman system, ten is shown by an **X**, while one hundred is shown by a **C**.

The earliest piece of writing that shows a date with tens and hundreds in separate columns, comes from Gujarat in India. The writing is dated AD 595. An 8th century example shows the number 330, shown with the zero written as a small circle.

For a long time, people thought that the decimal place system had been invented by the Arabs. It was usually referred to as the Arabic numeral system. But the Arabs called these numerals the 'Indian Art'.

The Arabs probably learned this 'art' from the Indians during the 8th century. During this time, Baghdad became the centre of learning in the Arab world. Here, Indian books were translated and Indian scholars gathered together. Later, the Europeans learned Indian numerals and the decimal place system from the Arabs.

I	1
II	2
III	3
IV	4
V	5
VI	6
VII	7
VIII	8
IX	9
X	10

The decimal numerals on the right could be used to solve complicated problems. Roman numerals, such as the ones on the left, couldn't.

Chandra Gupta's marriage

The wedding was about to begin. The great nobles and ladies from the courts of Magadha and Lichchhavis had gathered to watch. Chandra Gupta I and Princess Kumaradevi sat facing each other. Their marriage had been arranged by their parents to ensure that peace continued between their two states. But despite this, everyone knew that the couple would like one another as well, especially after they had spent some time together.

Marriages like this, arranged between the rulers of two states, could be as important to a country as fighting a war. It meant that the two countries would remain friends, or allies. Chandra Gupta I didn't come from a 'royal' family, but he was a strong and able leader. By marrying a princess of the Lichchhavis, an old, established tribe, Chandra Gupta would increase his political and military power.

Chandra Gupta was proud of his marriage to Princess Kumaradevi. Coins minted during his reign carried her image. And, because of its importance, her name is written in the Gupta family tree.

Chandra Gupta was the first important Gupta ruler. The Guptas ruled from AD 320 to about AD 540, during one of the most important periods in the history of Indian civilization.

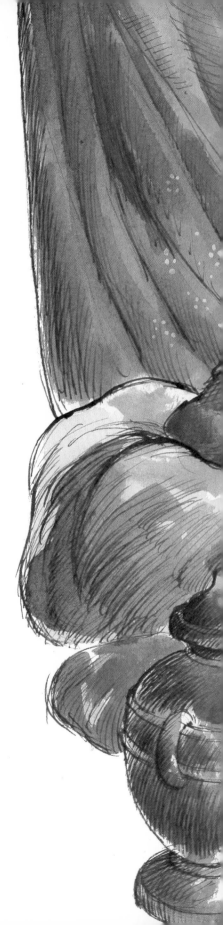

Working in stone

This beautifully sculpted temple is at Baroli, Rajasthan.

During the 5th century, there lived a Chinese Buddhist monk called Fa-hein. Between AD 405 and AD 411, Fa-hein spent six years travelling around India. Luckily for us, he kept a record of his travels. In this record he wrote how contented the people were and how well governed the country was.

During this time, India was a fairly peaceful and prosperous country. A large amount of trade was taking place between India, China and the West, and the wealth that this brought the country allowed the people to be creative. Painters, writers, sculptors and stonemasons were all able to find plenty of work, especially sculptors and stonemasons.

Many magnificent statues and temples were built during this period. Some of the finest Gupta sculptures can be found at Sarnath. These are images of the Buddha and they show him looking serene and compassionate.

Sculptors also carved images of their gods. A statue of a Hindu god may have looked like a human, but the god was shown to have four or eight arms. Each arm might have held a symbol of one of the god's special powers. Most of the Hindu sculptures were of the god Vishnu.

The Gupta temples were usually small, with flat roofs, and built of stone. They were dedicated to the various Hindu gods. The temple began with a shrine room in the middle. This is where the image of the god was placed. Outside this room was a smaller entrance room, and a porch. A courtyard surrounded the building.

Sometimes, other shrines were built inside the courtyard. The Vishnu temple at Deogarh had a small tower which rose above the shrine room.

This is a sculpture of the Buddha, from Sarnath.

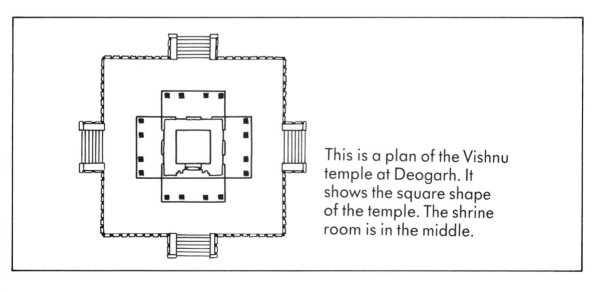

This is a plan of the Vishnu temple at Deogarh. It shows the square shape of the temple. The shrine room is in the middle.

Playing gods and kings

The actors glided smoothly across the polished stone floor. They moved like birds in flight. A drama teacher stood close by, watching his pupils. He had been teaching them the dancing steps for a new play which they were going to perform in front of a wealthy nobleman.

This form of drama began in India in ancient times. We can learn a great deal about it from a book called the 'Natyashastra', written by a brahmin called Bharata.

Bharata said that drama should be a mixture of singing, dancing and acting, and that it should imitate the actions of gods and kings. He also said that drama should offer the audience good advice, and make them feel strong and courageous. In many ways, these ideas are similar to those of ancient Greek drama. But Indian drama was different in one important way. The Greeks wrote many sad plays, or tragedies, but the early Indians much preferred a happy ending!

A traditional Indian play is divided into six parts. These are decoration, postures, which describe the way people stand, gestures, which describe the way people move, moods, words and music.

Bharata felt that dance was very important. He felt that a dancer should be able to make people feel particular emotions, or moods, such as sadness or joy. He called these moods 'rasas' and named nine of them. These were love, humour, pity, anger, terror, disgust, heroism, wonder and calmness of mind.

The theatre of ancient India has had a great influence on classical forms of dance and music in India. Many classical plays are still performed in India today.

anger

disgust

love

calmness of mind

Rasas, like the ones above, and finger movements, help the performer to express himself.

Shakuntala

The noblemen and women watched the actors carefully. They were enjoying the play, but it was very sad. Many of the women actually had tears in their eyes! The play was called 'Shakuntala'. It was written in about AD 400, during the reign of Chandra Gupta II, by a brilliant court poet and playwright called Kalidasa. Many wonderful works of art were created during this period.

This is the story of Shakuntala. One day, King Dushyanta went hunting in the woods where he saw a beautiful young girl called Shakuntala. Shakuntala was so lovely that the king instantly fell in love with her. He married her and lived with her in the forest, forgetting all about his duties at court.

After a time, King Dushyanta was recalled to his court by affairs of state. He left Shakuntala, promising to send for her later on. Soon, he seemed to forget all about her. This forgetfulness was caused by a curse put on Shakuntala by an angry teacher, or sage.

Shakuntala was heart-broken. She went to the court to show the king the ring he had given her. But it slipped from her finger and was swallowed by a fish. When she arrived, the king didn't recognise her. Shakuntala was terribly unhappy and she left the court. Not long afterwards, she gave birth to a baby boy.

Some time later, Shakuntala's ring was found by a fisherman. The ring was taken to the king. When the king recognised it, his memory returned. Some years later, he was united with his son and, finally, with Shakuntala.

Sushruta

Sushruta picked up the strangely shaped instruments and examined them carefully. He had performed this operation many times before, but he wanted to make sure that everything was clean and ready. Today, his patient was a soldier who had lost part of his nose in battle.

Skilfully, Sushruta used his instruments to cut some skin from the soldier's side. Then he shaped the skin to build up a new nose. The soldier would look terrible for a while, but in a few weeks, the cuts would heal and his nose would be almost as good as new.

This kind of surgery is called plastic surgery. Plastic surgery was often practised in ancient India. In fact, surgical operations have been carried out in India for over two thousand years.

Sushruta not only practised surgery, but wrote about it as well. His book, the 'Sushruta Samhita', was based on the teachings of Dhanvantari, who lived much earlier. It contains 184 chapters, 120 of which deal with surgery, 64 with medicine. The book describes five types of bones, eight kinds of operations, fourteen types of bandages, and 121 surgical instruments!

Sushruta also gave good advice to other surgeons. He said that all surgeons should shave off their beards and cut their nails. He insisted that they should take a bath before operating and wear clean, white clothes. He also suggested that patients should drink wine before an operation, as it would help to deaden the pain.

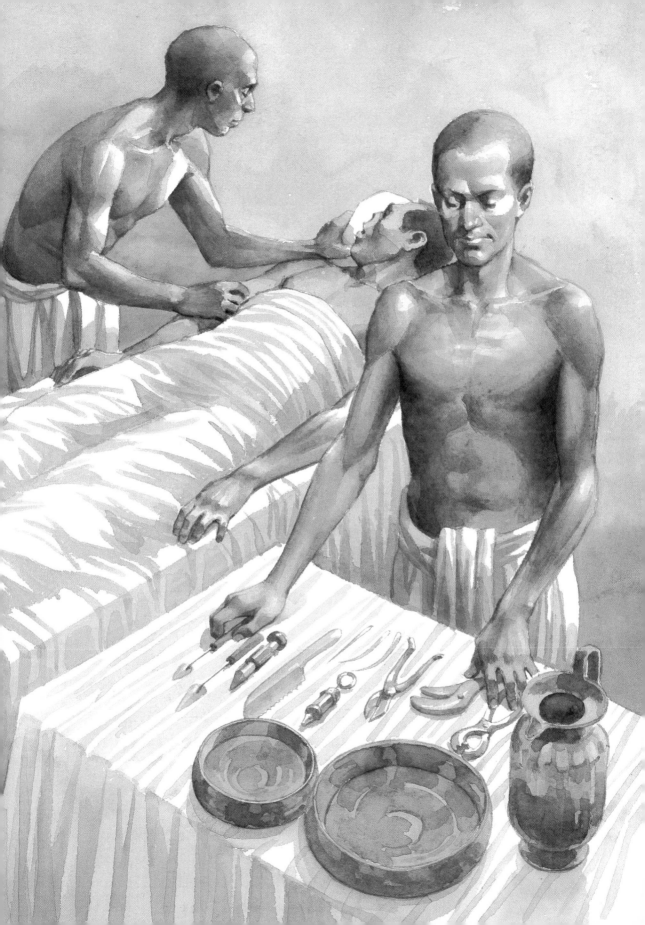

The Story of the Anklet

'The Story of the Anklet' is a Tamil poem written about fifteen hundred years ago. It is one of the greatest of the Tamil epic poems. Like the 'Mahabharata', it is very long, but it is written in the Tamil language rather than Sanskrit. Unlike the 'Mahabharata', it is a story of ordinary people with ordinary problems, and it doesn't have a happy ending.

We think that 'The Story of the Anklet', was written by Elangoadizhal. But we do not know for sure.

The story begins when Kovalan, the son of one wealthy merchant, marries Kannagi, the daughter of another. The two young people live happily together until Kovalan visits the court of the king. Here, he meets a dancer called Madhavi and falls in love with her. Kovalan spends all his time and money trying to please Madhavi, and soon forgets his own wife, Kannagi.

Eventually, Kovalan uses up all his money. He is forced to return home to Kannagi, who forgives him. Together, they decide to go to the great city of Madurai to start a new life.

In Madurai, Kannagi presents Kovalan with one of a pair of wonderful anklets to sell, so he can start a business.

Kovalan goes to the market place and sells one of the anklets to a jeweller. However, the Queen of Madurai has just been robbed of a similar anklet. The wicked jeweller tells the king that it is Kovalan who has stolen the queen's anklet. Poor Kovalan is arrested by the king and executed without trial.

Kannagi mourns her husband's death and then becomes very angry. She goes to the king and shows him the second anklet to prove her husband's innocence. The king realises how unjust he has been, and dies of guilt.

Kannagi is still angry. She condemns the city of Madurai, which goes up in flames. Luckily, though, the patron goddess of the city persuades her to take back her curse and the fire stops. But Kannagi is badly hurt in the fire, and dies.

Today, Kannagi is honoured as the goddess of all faithful and loyal wives.

Aryabhata

Aryabhata looked up at the Moon shining above his head, and at the night sky full of stars. He enjoyed watching the way in which the Moon and stars seemed to move across the sky. But Aryabhata was convinced that it was really the Earth that was moving, not the stars at all. He believed that the Earth had an invisible axis, or line, through its centre and that it turned on this axis like a great ball.

Aryabhata's ideas about the movements of the stars and planets were different from those of the other astronomers of his time. These men believed that the Earth was the centre of the solar system, and that the stars, Moon and Sun revolved around the Earth.

Aryabhata was born in AD 476. The study of the stars and planets, called astronomy, has been practised in India for more than two thousand years. This science was called 'jyotisha'. At first, it was used mainly to arrange the dates and times of sacrifices. Later, Indian astronomers might possibly have been influenced by those who studied Greek astronomy.

Early Indian astronomers didn't have telescopes as we do. They had to rely on the accuracy of their eyesight to watch the night sky. Therefore, they only knew about the five planets nearest to the Earth — Mercury, Venus, Mars, Jupiter and Saturn.

But these astronomers were able to make accurate measurements, partly because they used the decimal system of numerals. And their knowledge of mathematics was advanced. Aryabhata was a great mathematician. His value for π, or 'pi', of 3.1416, is still used today.

Aryabhata often challenged popular beliefs and arrived at correct explanations for things. For example, he was correct about what caused an eclipse of the Sun. Hundreds of years later, Aryabhata's ideas were proved to be right.

King Harsha

The young king stood sternly beside the huge grey elephant. The boy was only sixteen.

Harsha was hardly old enough to be king, but anyone who saw him or talked to him knew that he would be a great ruler. He would grow to be wise, brave and intelligent.

Harsha's court poet, Bana, wrote a book about Harsha's life, called 'Harshacharita'. A Chinese traveller, called Hsuan Tsang, wrote about how Indian people lived during Harsha's reign. From these two writers, we can learn how Harsha ruled a great empire that stretched from Gujarat to Bengal, and how he was strong enough to control the kings in neighbouring lands. He only let them rule if they proved to be loyal to him.

Harsha felt that he could only rule his kingdom well if he saw what was going on with his own eyes. So he travelled from one province to another, listening to the complaints of his subjects and making sure that his laws were obeyed.

Harsha often held 'audiences', or meetings, in a travelling pavilion, or tent, which would be set up by the roadside. Then, gorgeously dressed courtiers, proud officials, attendants, Buddhist monks and brahmins who travelled with Harsha would gather round this decorated pavilion. When the meeting was over, everyone would hustle and bustle to get the great procession on the move again.

Harsha was very loyal and generous to his friends. He loved books and plays and actually wrote three dramas himself. In AD 647, he died and the great kingdom he had built fell apart. Sadly, he hadn't left a son to rule the kingdom after him.

This is the Kailashanath temple at Ellora.

The Kailashanath temple

The craftsman chiselled carefully around his sculpture, adding the finishing touches. The figure was beginning to look smooth and fine. Then the sculptor ran his fingers along the figure's arm and took a step back to view the whole work.

All around him, sculptors and craftsmen were finishing their work. The great temple on which they had laboured for so many years was almost complete.

The Kailashanath temple at Ellora is one of the most magnificent Hindu temples in India. It was dug into solid rock, or excavated, to a depth of thirty metres. And archaeologists think that almost twenty thousand tonnes of rock had to be taken out and moved away from the site during the excavations. This great work was created during the 8th century for the Rashtrakuta king, Krishna I.

Sculptures like these decorate the temple walls.

This wall looks as if it has grown from the rock.

The democratic king

There was a great deal of bustle going on all round the docks. Carpenters and sailmakers, sailors and traders were rushing this way and that, trying to get the ships of the fleet ready for sailing.

The great king, Rajaraja Chola, was planning to attack nearby islands. Trade was very important to the Chola Empire. The king was going to use his navy to protect his Chola traders from their Arab competitors along the South-east Asian sea-routes, and from pirates along the Malabar coast.

The Chola kings had been ruling in some parts of southern India since about AD 100. As time went on, they grew stronger. By about AD 850, they had taken over neighbouring kingdoms and become the most feared power in the south.

Rajaraja was the greatest of the Chola kings. He was a fair and honourable leader in his dealings with his subjects. His government was run by capable administrators who advised him on many things. Royal orders were only carried out after the administrators had agreed to them.

Other officials helped the king run the empire on different levels, and very small settlements, like villages, were allowed to manage their own affairs.

Rajaraja is often thought of as a democratic king. A true democracy means that the power to run a country lies entirely with the people. Rajaraja's state wasn't a true democracy, but his people were able to have some say in the government's decisions.

Owning the land

During medieval times, in the southern kingdoms of India, the land was owned by the king. He could give grants to his officers or to brahmins, which entitled them to the revenue from the land, or he could have the land cultivated by small-scale farmers and landlords. Usually, the king chose the second way.

During the reign of the Chola kings, people who worked on the land often lived in local villages. In each village, there were homes, gardens, irrigation works, cattle enclosures, waste lands and a village common. There might also be a forest surrounding the village, a temple with its own grounds, and cremation grounds where the dead were cremated.

An assembly called a 'sabha' looked after the running of the brahmadeya villages, or villages of brahmins. The sabha dealt with all the main concerns of the village, such as irrigation, the punishment of crime, keeping records and keeping a count of the inhabitants. The village courts dealt with simple crimes, while more serious crimes were tried in courts held by government officials. The king could always have the final word if he wished.

A similar assembly to the sabha, called an 'ur', looked after the running of the ordinary villages. Sometimes, a village had both a sabha and an ur.

Only people who paid taxes were eligible to become members of an assembly, or to help run one. Agricultural workers were excluded. The leader of the village, or village headman, was the link between the village and the government. Representatives of different villages met in a special assembly, which was called a 'nadu'.

This system of government gave the people of southern India a say in how their affairs should be run. It was a kind of democracy, a very modern sort of government for its time.

Temples and bronzes

During the reign of the Chola kings, huge temples were built all over southern India. These were to show devotion to the god Shiva, whom the people worshipped. The great temple at Tanjore, for example, was like a small town. If an enemy attacked, it could be used as a fortress. Inside, there was room for over two hundred attendants, fifty-seven musicians, hundreds of priests and readers of the holy text, and four hundred dancing girls.

At the Brihadeswara temple at Tanjore, there are many paintings and sculptures of dance postures.

This is a statue of Shiva as Nataraja, the god of dance.

The cost of maintaining such a rich and magnificent spectacle was met by revenues collected from the villages, as well as by offerings of gold, silver and precious stones. Sometimes, the temple acted as a bank and lent money to village assemblies or other similar groups. The people of southern India also made beautiful bronze statues of gods and royalty. The craftsmen who made these statues were highly skilled.

These delicate figures from southern India are made out of bronze.

The fire families

A long time ago, a wise man called Vasishtha owned a very special cow. This cow was called a 'kamadhenu'. A kamadhenu could grant any wish its owner asked of it.

One day, Vasishtha's special cow was stolen. Vasishtha was naturally very upset and tried to find out who was the thief. Soon, he discovered that the guilty person was another wise man, called Vishvamitra.

Vasishtha was furious. Immediately, he went to the sacrificial fire at Mount Abu and made an offering there. At once, a mighty hero sprang out of the flames of the fire and set off in search of the cow.

When the cow was found and returned to its rightful owner, Vasishtha, he was overjoyed. He called the hero Paramara, which means 'slayer of the enemy'.

Paramara's descendants were known as the
Paramara clan, which became one of the great
Rajput clans. The Rajputs were divided into
different tribes and clans, and four of these
were especially important. They were the
Pratiharas, the Chauhans, the Chalukyas and
the Paramaras. They rose to importance during
the 9th and 10th centuries. The story of
Paramara is only a myth. The clans may
actually have been descended from the Huns
and other groups of people who had settled
down in different parts of northern and
western India.

Each one of these clans claimed that their
people were descended from a mythical being,
like Paramara. Because this mythical being
had risen out of the sacrificial fire near Mount
Abu, they called themselves the 'Agnikula', or
fire family.

This miniature shows how
the Rajputs dressed. They
wore flowing robes and
magnificent turbans.

Kings and lords

The soldier stood silently in front of the king and bowed very low. Then he began to back away. He had been a brave and successful warrior and was now getting his reward. He had been given large areas of good land by the king, with lots of peasants to work on it. Soon, he would be very powerful indeed.

In the period when the Guptas and Harsha ruled, kings often used to give their officers money as payment. After that time, some kings, especially in the Rajput states, gave their officers and friends land instead. And they gave them the right to collect taxes from the villages in that land.

Under this system, the chiefs who had been given land had to perform certain duties for their king. They had to pay him some of the tax money collected from the villages. They had to keep soldiers to fight for the king if he needed them. And they had to attend the king's court when they were summoned.

The king granted his chiefs certain privileges. They were allowed to give themselves grand titles, and they could sit on magnificent thrones and ride in special covered chairs, or palanquins.

Some chiefs had more land than they needed or wanted. These chiefs gave part of their land to the less important chiefs, who gave money and soldiers in return.

This system worked rather like the feudal systems in England and Japan. But it wasn't quite the same.

Most of the chiefs who were given land came from the military castes. But the king also granted land to brahmins. The brahmins didn't have to pay taxes or keep soldiers.

The land was cultivated by peasants. They had to pay taxes on almost everything, from looms to cattle. They were nearly always very poor. Because they had no power, they had no alternative but to pay what their chief demanded from them. Their welfare depended upon how considerate the chief was.

1. King
2. Chief
3. Brahmin
4. Lesser chiefs
5. Peasants

Mahmud of Ghazni

Mahmud of Ghazni marched into the silent temple of Somnath. Inside, it was dark except for a huge idol in the middle of the temple, lit by jewelled chandeliers. Mahmud stopped and stared. The wonderful figure seemed to hang suspended in the air. Mahmud was a Muslim and so forbidden by his religion to worship idols, but he was fascinated.

Mahmud ordered his men to seize all the treasure they could find. Then he looked at the idol again. How did it stay up? Perhaps it was held in position by magnetic loadstones in the canopy! Mahmud ordered his men to remove some of the stones and, as they did so, the great idol began to tilt. Soon, it was resting on the ground. Mahmud of Ghazni left the temple.

Mahmud was a Muslim king who ruled a small country north-west of India, called Ghazni. He was the first of a number of Turkish rulers to invade northern India, bringing with them the Muslim religion. He wanted to conquer lands to the west, in Central Asia, because of the important trade-routes between China and the Mediterranean. And he was greedy for gold and riches. He knew he could get these if he raided north-west India. Then he could use the treasures he had seized from India to help build up a vast empire.

From about AD 1000, Mahmud raided India regularly, year after year. His troops acted fast and efficiently. They raided and plundered Mathura, Thanesar, Kanauj and other towns, as well as Somnath.

Mahmud made sure that his soldiers arrived at harvest time so the Indian farmers had to feed them. This made the farmers hate the raiders even more.

Mahmud lived until 1030. As well as being a soldier, he was a patron of the arts. The great scholar, Albiruni, accompanied him to India and stayed there for a number of years. Albiruni wrote an important work on India's religions, science, society, philosophy and culture.

72

The stolen princess

A long time ago, according to legend, a beautiful princess called Sangyukta lived in Kanauj. She was in love with a handsome and daring king called Prithviraja. But her father, Jayachandra, hated this king and wouldn't let them get married.

One day, Jayachandra decided to hold a Swayamvara gathering for his daughter. Here, by tradition, she would choose a husband from among the gathered princes. He invited all the princes in India to attend, except Prithviraja. And he stood a clay statue of Prithviraja by the door, in the position of doorkeeper. This was very insulting.

Soon, the ceremony began. All the princes stood waiting for the princess to make her choice. But Sangyukta paid no attention to any of them. Instead, she picked up a garland of jasmine and gently placed it around the neck of the statue.

The gathering broke up in noise and confusion. Jayachandra was furious! But before he could do anything, the real Prithviraja suddenly appeared from where he had been hiding, to steal away his bride. He rushed up to the princess and carried her away on his horse. They fled together to his own kingdom where they were married.

Prithviraja was one of the many kings of northern India who called themselves Rajputs. The legend of this daring deed was just the kind of thing that the Rajputs enjoyed hearing about. They loved fighting and adventure. And they created a whole way of living which allowed them to wage war at the slightest excuse. In fact, the Rajputs were always at war with each other. This meant that they could never build a strong empire or unite to defend themselves against invaders.

Rajput women were taught to admire bravery. They would ride and hunt with their husbands. And a woman had to be ready to die if her husband was killed. Rajput children began to learn how to ride, shoot and use other military skills when they were very young. Court singers sang songs about the princes' heroic deeds, and about those of their ancestors. The songs made the listeners want to be brave and strong, and to protect the weak and the helpless.

The Slave Dynasty

Qutb-ud-din watched as his Ghurid cavalry stormed across the plain. Each rider carried a crossbow which he could fire at the gallop.

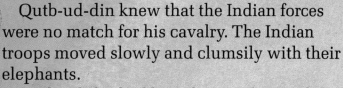

Qutb-ud-din knew that the Indian forces were no match for his cavalry. The Indian troops moved slowly and clumsily with their elephants.

Qutb-ud-din had been born a slave. While he was still young, he was enrolled in the army of Sultan Muhammad of Ghur. Qutb-ud-din proved to be a very good soldier, and soon he had become the loyal slave-lieutenant of the sultan.

In 1182, Qutb-ud-din followed Sultan Muhammad on a raid into north-west India. Qutb-ud-din's soldiers rode through the pass at Gomal and quickly defeated the rulers of Sind. But Muhammad wanted more than just to raid and loot. He wanted to establish his own kingdom in India.

Sultan Muhammad moved east and fought bloody battles with the Rajput princes. The Rajputs defended their lands stubbornly. But by 1194, Muhammad and his lieutenant, Qutb-ud-din, had taken many lands, including the Kingdom of Delhi.

In 1206, Muhammad was assassinated and Qutb-ud-din proclaimed himself sultan in India. No one opposed him. He became the first of several lines of Delhi sultans whose reigns lasted for over three hundred years. The dynasty he established came to be known as the 'Slave Dynasty'. Now the Turks were no longer just raiders. They had become a settled people, fitting into the way of life in India.

March to Daulatabad

The column of noblemen and courtiers wound through the lush green forest. The dense canopy of trees made the air seem dark and heavy, and the heat from the midday sun was almost unbearable. But Sultan Muhammad Tughluq wanted to get to Daulatabad as soon as possible. He wouldn't let his court and people stop.

In 1327, Muhammad Tughluq decided to move the capital from Delhi to Daulatabad in the Deccan. This city had earlier been called Deogiri. Muhammad thought he could control his empire better from a more central position. He ordered all the inhabitants of Delhi to leave their homes and trek south, and set up home in Daulatabad. This involved a difficult journey of 1,500 kilometres.

When the people eventually got to Daulatabad, they found it uncomfortable and hot, and there was very little water. Muhammad Tughluq soon realized that it wasn't such a good idea after all. So he moved the capital back to Delhi again!

This was just one of Muhammad's ingenious ideas that failed. Another was a new currency to replace silver and gold coins. But that failed too, because people made so many false coins that the currency became worthless.

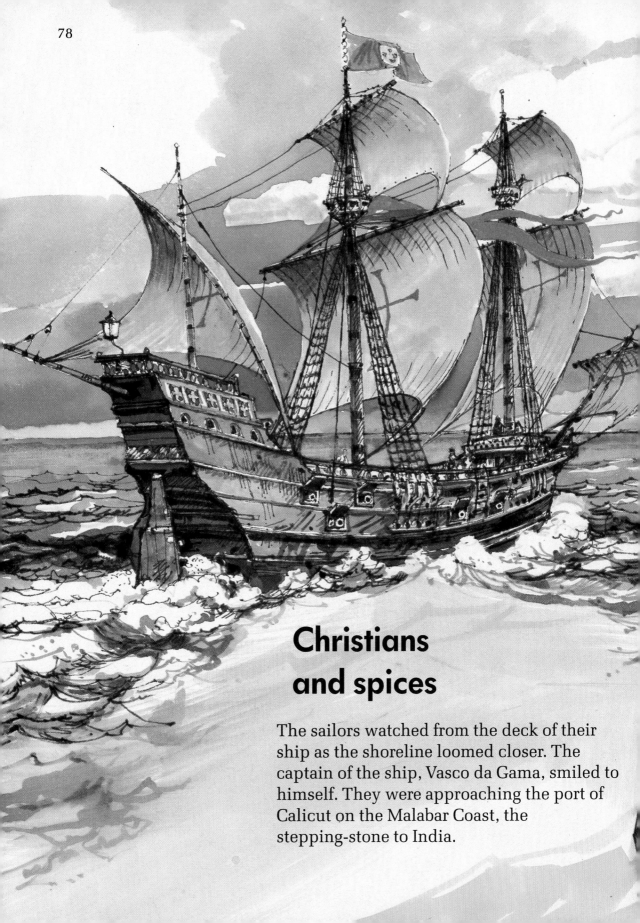

Christians and spices

The sailors watched from the deck of their ship as the shoreline loomed closer. The captain of the ship, Vasco da Gama, smiled to himself. They were approaching the port of Calicut on the Malabar Coast, the stepping-stone to India.

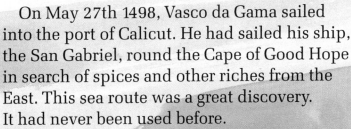

On May 27th 1498, Vasco da Gama sailed into the port of Calicut. He had sailed his ship, the San Gabriel, round the Cape of Good Hope in search of spices and other riches from the East. This sea route was a great discovery. It had never been used before.

Calicut was a very busy port. It was well known to Arab and Chinese traders, and its ruler, the Zamorin, was one of the richest princes along the coast. Vasco da Gama told the Zamorin that he had come to find 'Christians and Spices'. The Zamorin knew that trade with foreign visitors would bring him more profit in taxes, so he welcomed the Western merchants.

The San Gabriel carried twenty guns on board, but Vasco da Gama didn't know how successful he might be if he got into trouble with the traders in this strange port. So he ordered his men to pay whatever price the Calicut merchants asked for their goods.

The Portuguese loaded their ships with Indian spices — cardamom, cinnamon and cloves — which were very much in demand in Europe.

When Vasco da Gama returned to Portugal, he managed to sell his goods for sixty times what the two-year expedition had cost. This was an enormous profit! The news spread through Lisbon, the Portuguese capital, and eleven more Portuguese ships were built, ready to sail to India.

Vasco da Gama's journey began a new period of trade between Europe and India. The Portuguese dominated Europe's trade with India for over a hundred years.

Vijayanagar

The cavalry of King Krishna Deva Raya formed an important part of his army. But he needed more horses, and good horses weren't easy to find in India. So the king invited Portuguese traders to the royal city of Vijayanagar. They would provide him with the best animals.

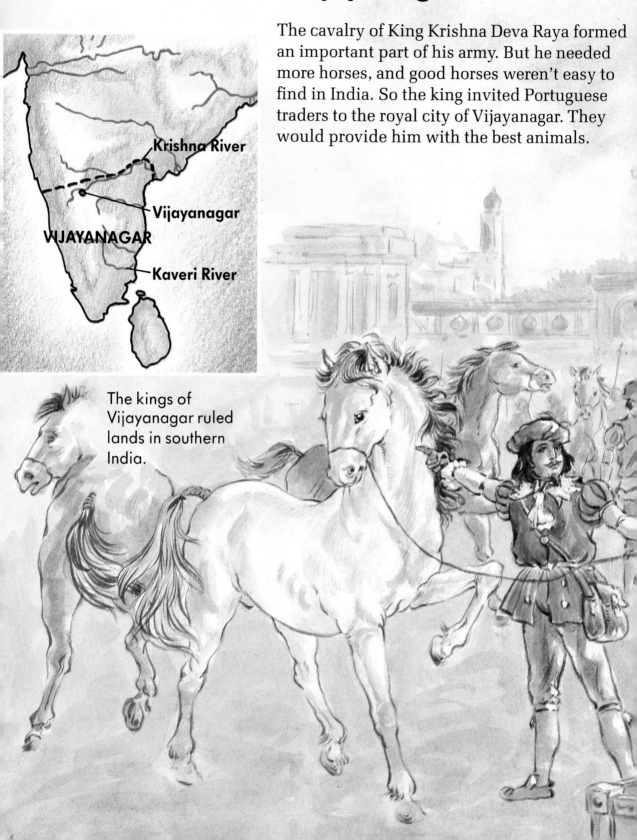

Krishna River

Vijayanagar

VIJAYANAGAR

Kaveri River

The kings of Vijayanagar ruled lands in southern India.

The Portuguese admired King Krishna Deva Raya, who was a scholar in Sanskrit and Telugu, and a warrior. They even wanted to join him in his battles against the other Indian kingdoms. But although Krishna Deva Raya wanted the Portuguese to supply him with horses, he didn't want to become their friend in battle.

Krishna Deva Raya's kingdom of Vijayanagar lay in the Deccan, and in parts of southern India. It had developed since 1336, when Prince Harihara had become king of Hastinavati. This prince was a fine ruler and he had soon made the kingdom the strongest in the south.

After defeating many enemies, Harihara built the city of Vijayanagar as his capital, which means City of Victory. Later, the whole kingdom became known as Vijayanagar.

As Vijayanagar became stronger and more important, its enemies grew in number. One of Harihara's successors was forced to increase the size of the army in order to protect the city. He took more money in taxes, hired Turkish soldiers, and strengthened his cavalry with new horses. These were imported into the country by Arab traders.

This trade in horses continued into Krishna Deva Raya's reign. But now, the traders were Portuguese, not Arabs. They began to grow rich from their dealings in the great city.

Devotion

Kabir sat quietly at his loom, listening to the songs of one of his followers. He began to think about his work as a teacher, about the idea of human brotherhood and love. He believed in one god whom people called by different names.

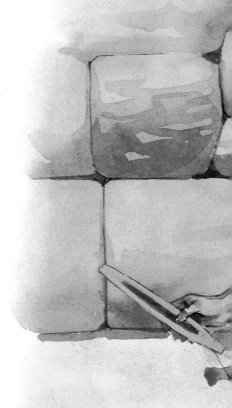

The idea of all attaining salvation through 'Bhakti', or devotion, had arisen centuries ago. Lord Krishna taught many things. One of the most important of these was the idea of love, which he called 'devotion' or 'Bhakti'. Krishna explained that if an evil person learned to love his god with all his heart, he would be regarded as good, even if he had been wicked in the past. And women, workmen, peasants and the poor of all castes, could attain salvation through 'Bhakti'. Until then, the traditional message of Hinduism had been that only the upper castes in society could hope for salvation. The saints of South India preached devotion to Vishnu and Shiva. The idea of 'Bhakti' later spread to North India, and this became a popular religious movement.

The Bhakti movement was against religious narrow-mindedness. It helped to bring Hindus and Muslims together.

Bhakti teachers didn't use the traditional language of Sanskrit. Instead, they wrote and taught in local languages so that their ideas were more easily understood by the ordinary people.

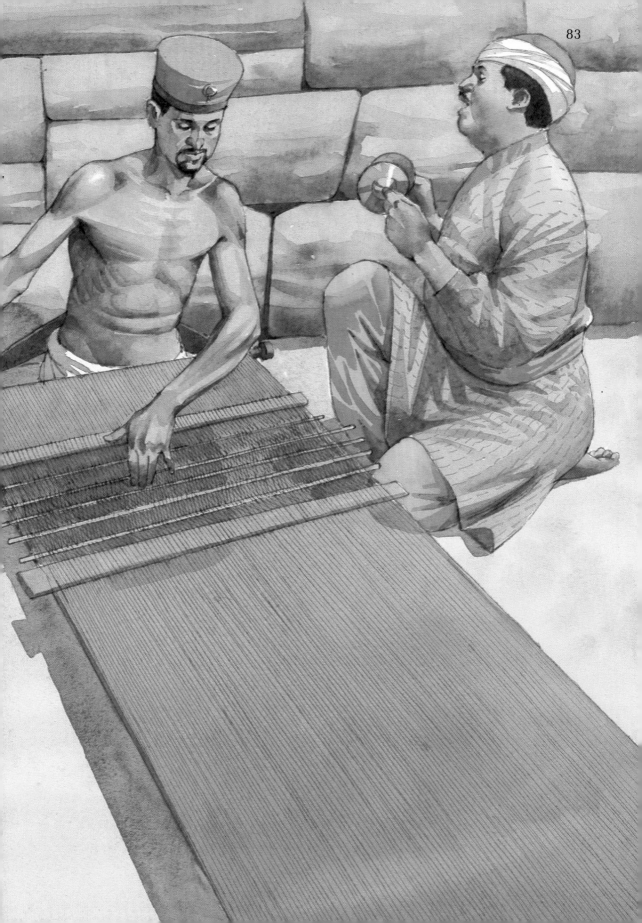

Guru Nanak

Guru Nanak thought long and hard about his future. He wanted to do what he believed to be right, which was to teach people that religious differences between Hindus and Muslims should end.

In 1500, Nanak left his wife and three children and joined the Sufis. The Sufis were a religious group who shared many of his beliefs. He didn't stay with them for very long, but began to travel through India and to other countries, teaching his ideas.

Guru Nanak taught that there is just one God, and that statues and paintings of gods shouldn't be worshipped. True religion, according to him, consisted in devotion to one God, and reciting His name with love. He was opposed to rituals and all that created divisions among men.

When Nanak returned from his travels, he went back to live with his family in a village in the Punjab. There, he gathered disciples, or followers, around him and taught them his beliefs. In particular, he taught that they shouldn't envy riches or allow their feelings to interfere with clear thinking. He encouraged them to lead good and peaceful lives.

Many people began to follow Nanak's teachings. When he died, his followers created a separate religion based on his teachings, which they called the Sikh religion. Sikh means disciple.

Today, there are about fourteen million Sikhs in India, who live in the Punjab and in other parts of India.

The holiest of Sikh shrines is the Golden Temple at Amritsar.

The Sikh symbol is made up of two curved swords, a double-edged dagger and a discus. It stands for bravery and spiritual power.

Babur
the king

Babur was delighted! The workmen were bustling around and listening to him, following his instructions. They were constructing a water-garden just like the ones he used to enjoy so much in his homeland. Babur was looking forward to feeling cool and comfortable in his garden.

Babur was born in the small country of Farghana, in Trans-Oxiana, Central Asia. He was descended from Timur, the great Turkish warrior, and from the Mongol leader, Changez Khan.

In 1494, Babur had become king when he was only eleven years old. Soon, he was threatened by a strong, young Uzbeg chief called Shaibani Khan, who finally drove him out of his country. Babur was a brave and clever leader. He spent many years trying to win back his country and, by 1504, he had built up a strong kingdom in what is now called Afghanistan.

Meanwhile, in northern India, local chiefs had grown discontented with their ruler, the Sultan of Delhi, and wanted to get rid of him. Babur knew this. Also, because his ancestor, Timur, had once conquered Delhi, Babur felt that he had the right to take the sultan's place.

So, in 1523, Babur began to raid northern India. By 1526, his army was strong enough to defeat the Sultan of Delhi. Babur took control of the Sultan of Delhi's territories and became the first of the Mughal emperors.

The local chiefs hoped that Babur might return to his own kingdom as soon as the hot Indian summer came. But Babur wanted to start his own empire in India. The Rajput princes gathered an army together to fight him, but they were defeated. Babur became the unchallenged ruler.

Babur wasn't just a great soldier and statesman but also a man of learning. He read Arabic and Persian as well as Turkish, and he was a great lover of poetry. He wrote his life-story, which was called the 'Babur Nama'. In 1530, Babur died.

Village life

All morning, the farmer drove the bullocks up and down the small piece of land that he worked, ploughing furrow after furrow. When the ploughing was done, he would plant millet and other crops there. Like all the other farmers in the village, he grew most of the food that his family needed. There would be just enough left over to trade for other goods.

When the farmer had woken early that morning, the sun was rising and it was time to go to work. Quietly, he got up from his sleeping-mat and went outside to wash in a nearby pool. Then he returned to his hut and tied a turban round his head to protect himself from the fierce heat of the sun.

After eating the morning meal his wife had prepared for him, the farmer walked to the field with his two bullocks and hitched them to a plough. The plough was made from a strong wooden stock with an iron blade.

At midday, the farmer rested under a shady tree. Then he trudged back to his work. It was a long day and very tiring, but in the evening, the farmer would be able to relax a little and talk to the other men of the village. He was a member of the village council and helped run the affairs of the little community. This evening, the council would discuss the fair that was due to arrive in just a few days' time.

At the fair, the farmer might hear stories of the king's wars. But he wasn't very interested. He knew that some men were born to be soldiers and others to cultivate the land. One man couldn't do both.

Akbar the unifier

Akbar sat and listened patiently to the priests and holy men around him. There were Portuguese Catholics, Hindus, Muslims and Jains in the group. They were all talking brilliantly about their different beliefs and philosophies.

Akbar wanted to unite his country. He wondered how it could possibly be done. There were so many different religions in India! He knew that his people wouldn't accept just one religion, even if he ordered them to. There had to be another solution to the problem.

Akbar was the greatest of the Mughal emperors. As the grandson of Babur, he was a brave, strong and able leader. And unlike the many rulers before him, he was also open-minded and willing to listen to other people's points of view.

Akbar assembled a set of beliefs drawn from many religions. This came to be called the Divine Faith, or 'Din-i-Illahi'. Akbar made himself the head of this faith. Although Akbar naturally expected obedience from his followers, he didn't force his religious ideas on anyone.

Akbar realised that, as a Muslim, he mustn't ignore his Hindu subjects. He stopped the unwelcome payment of the pilgrim tax at the Hindu holy cities. And he ended the 'jaziyah', a tax that had to be paid by anybody who wasn't a Muslim. Finally, Akbar placed Hindu nobles in high positions in his government, and he married Hindu princesses himself.

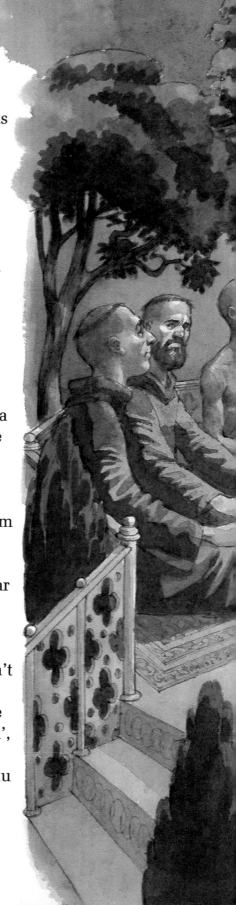

Many people have thought that Akbar's ideas were the result of an old man's wandering mind. In fact, he was only forty. His religious ideas were well thought out and they helped to unite his empire. Above all, Akbar was respected by both Hindus and Muslims alike.

City of Victory

The young man wiped the sweat from his face and sighed. He had spent a hard day in the hot sun. After one more load, his work would be done. Slowly, he bent down and filled his basket with six or seven more bricks. Then he lifted it onto his turbaned head and walked steadily up a steep ramp towards the masons who were working on the partly-built wall.

Later that evening, the young man strolled along one of the city's newly-paved streets. In the sunset, the city looked magnificent! He was very proud to be working there, even though the work was hard.

The city was called Fatehpur Sikri, or the City of Victory. It was built on the orders of Akbar in honour of a Sufi saint called Salim Chishti. The saint had promised Akbar that he would have a son who would start a long line of kings to rule the kingdom. The promise had been fulfilled. And in 1570, Akbar had begun work on the city.

Akbar directed the work on the city himself. It grew to a huge size. Near the centre of the city stood what is now called the Jodh Bai palace. A mosque was built at the tomb of Salim Chishti. To enter the city, visitors had to pass through a magnificent victory gate made of marble and sandstone, called the Buland Darwaza.

Many people thought that the city would be a busy centre for hundreds of years to come. But, after only fourteen years it was no longer used as the capital. It is likely that its water supply wasn't adequate.

A lady in power

The huge, swaying elephants moved slowly through the jungle, their riders perched high on their backs. Ahead, a tiger crouched in the dense undergrowth. The elephants began to move quickly forwards through the trees.

Suddenly, a shot rang out. Before the tiger was able to move, it fell to the ground. The elephants came to a standstill. One of the riders held a smoking rifle in her hands. She looked very pleased with herself. She was Nur Jahan, the wife of Emperor Jahangir, and as good a shot as any man!

Nur Jahan was a Persian lady. She had married a Persian officer of the Mughal Empire called Sher Afghan, but he had died and left her a widow. Four years later, Emperor Jahangir had met the beautiful Nur Jahan at a bazaar and decided to marry her.

The emperor's new wife was very talented and well educated. She wrote poetry in Persian, embroidered with silk thread, and designed jewellery and carpets. But she was also strong and energetic and loved to hunt tigers from the backs of elephants.

Nur Jahan was very ambitious. She wasn't content simply to be an emperor's bride. Soon, she began to take part in the running of the empire. The emperor was quite happy to let her do as she wished, and this included giving high posts in the government to her father and brother.

This system worked quite well until the emperor's children grew up and became powerful. Then Nur Jahan became worried that one of them, Shah Jahan, was becoming too ambitious. So she helped his rivals. Shah Jahan rebelled and later the emperor, his father, was imprisoned by one of his own generals.

Nur Jahan was able to free the emperor, but his health was poor and he died soon afterwards. Shah Jahan succeeded to the throne, and Nur Jahan realized that she could no longer influence the court. So from then on, she took no further part in politics.

Gifts from Persia

Any young man who wanted to work in the emperor's government in Mughal India had to have good knowledge of one language in particular. This language was Persian. Persian was the language of the Mughal administrators and of the Hindu nobles at some of the Rajput courts.

The Persian language was brought to India by the Turks during the 13th century, when they established the Sultanate of Delhi. Persian was the court language of the Delhi Sultanate.

During this period, architecture was influenced by Persian ideas, as well as by ideas from Central Asia and Arabia. Also, some of the best Persian literature was produced.

Indian miniatures like this painting were influenced by the work of Persian artists.

This wall painting shows the kind of Persian clothes that became fashionable in Mughal India.

The Mughals were enchanted by Persian culture. Persia was a great empire during Mughal times. It was powerful but it was also a great centre for learning, literature and the arts. The Mughals enjoyed Persian ways so much that they began to adopt them. They studied the Persian language, read Persian books and admired Persian art. Palaces and great buildings became a mixture of Hindu and Persian elements of style and decoration.

Hindu rulers also enjoyed Persian culture. All the great nobles in a Rajput court spoke Persian and knew about that country's paintings and architecture.

This was especially good for India, as it formed a link between Hindu and Muslim peoples, and helped them to understand each other better. Even the clothes that people wore were Persian in style. Fashionable lords and ladies wore clothes that would have been acceptable in a Persian court, as well as in their own.

At this time, the culture that developed was a mixture of Persian and Central Asian traditions and earlier Hindu traditions.

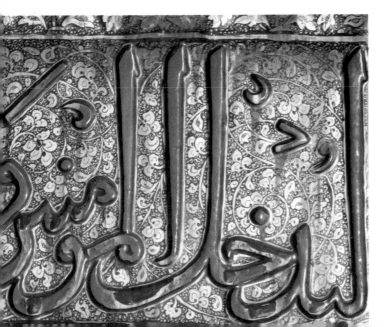

This beautiful Persian wall tile is decorated with Arabic writing, or script.

Miniature world

The Mughal emperors of India were good soldiers, but they also enjoyed literature, music and art.

Humayun, the son of Babur, admired Persian paintings. When he lived at Kabul, he encouraged Persian painters to live there. Akbar also admired their work. When he became emperor, he created a school for them, encouraging Persian and Indian masters to work together.

Another emperor, Jahangir, was skilled enough to identify the work of each individual painter, in a painting done by six or seven painters.

In 1567, Akbar ordered his artists to illustrate the 'Hamza Nama', a book about Amir Hamza, a hero of early Islam. Akbar liked the brilliant colours used by the Persian painters, but he felt that the paintings were stiff and formal. He wanted his court painters to produce works that combined Persian colour with Indian ideas and images, full of movement and energy.

The illustrations in the 'Hamza Nama' have a great deal of action and many bright colours, and the book contains fine drawings of architecture and landscape. In time, the Persian elements gradually became part of the paintings of Indian scenes, Indian landscape and Indian plants and animals.

Today, we call this style of painting the Mughal style. Because many of the paintings are quite small, they are known as miniatures. Mughal miniatures are often displayed in museums where they can still be seen.

These are European naval mercenaries from the Akbar Nama.

This is the Emperor Akbar, out hunting.

Animals, such as this zebra, were favourite subjects used by painters of miniatures.

The spice trade

Queen Elizabeth I of England carefully read through the charter before signing it. Under this order, eighty merchants from London had formed themselves into a trading group called the East India Company. They had collected £50,000 to pay for ships to travel to India, hoping to make huge profits from a trade in spices and silks.

In the East, the Portuguese and Dutch had already developed a flourishing trade in spices, and now they controlled most of the market. The English merchants decided to look elsewhere. They turned to India, where the spice trade wasn't so good, but where they could buy textiles.

At first, the East India Company found trading with India difficult. The Portuguese and Dutch had already established themselves, and had been preventing English traders to enter the market through their influence with Indian rulers.

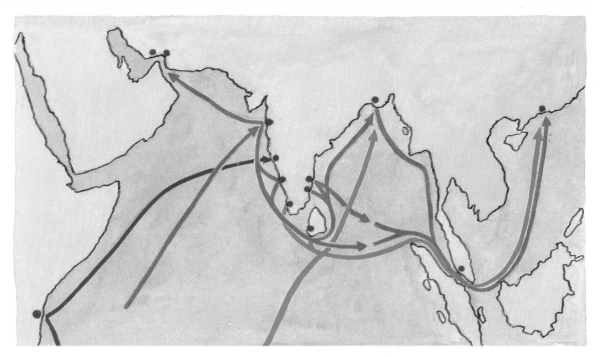

This map shows the trade routes to India.

In 1612, the English defeated a number of Portuguese ships in a naval battle, close to Surat in the Sually estuary. After this the Mughal rulers granted the English traders the right to establish trading posts in Surat. The Mughals wanted to use the English against the Portuguese naval power on the Indian sea coast.

In 1615, Sir Thomas Roe led an embassy to Emperor Jahangir's court. The East India Company was given permission to set up trading posts throughout the Mughal empire. In return, the English agreed to protect Indian merchant ships and pilgrim travellers from the threat of the Portuguese. Within a few years, the Portuguese control on India's trade with Europe came to an end.

Shah Jahan

Mumtaz Mahal

Shrine to love

At Agra Fort, the old emperor, Shah Jahan, sat quietly in his favourite place. He gazed through the evening twilight at a building that stood nearby. He thought it was the most beautiful building anyone had ever seen. Made out of white marble, the building glowed in the evening sun with a magical, soft, pink light. This building was called the Taj Mahal.

Shah Jahan had married a beautiful girl called Mumtaz Mahal. He had loved her deeply and they had fourteen children. Mumtaz Mahal went everywhere with her husband. She accompanied him on long journeys, and even into battle. She grew very tired and weak. After her fourteenth child, Mumtaz died. She was only thirty-nine.

Shah Jahan was so distressed by his wife's death that he had a magnificent tomb, called the Taj Mahal, built in her memory. It had taken twenty thousand labourers and more than twenty years to complete.

Shah Jahan was the greatest builder of all the Mughal emperors, and he will always be remembered for his love of the arts, especially architecture. His other great buildings include the Red Fort and the Jama Masjid, in Delhi. But the Taj Mahal is his most famous work. Today, people travel from all over the world to see it.

Shivaji's escape

Shivaji was a leader of the Marathas, a people who lived in central India. He was a very clever leader and highly skilled at guerilla warfare. The Mughal emperor, Aurangzeb, tried to make him into a Mughal officer, but Shivaji refused to accept the position and was arrested.

Shivaji paced up and down the length of his badly lit prison. He was being held at the court of Aurangzeb and there were burly, stern-faced guards standing outside his door. Shivaji thought of his people and how he wanted to be with them fighting the enemy.

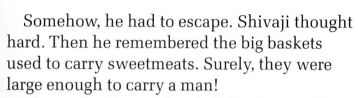

Somehow, he had to escape. Shivaji thought hard. Then he remembered the big baskets used to carry sweetmeats. Surely, they were large enough to carry a man!

The crafty Shivaji decided that he would send a basket of sweetmeats to the brahmins of Agra every day, as a present. He did this for some time.

Then one day, he lifted the lids of two baskets, removed some of the boxes and crawled inside with his son in their place. Carefully, the two hideaways covered themselves with boxes of sweetmeats and settled down to wait. It was a tight fit!

In no time, the baskets were carried out of the fort. The Maratha leader waited for the right moment, then he and his son leapt from the baskets and made their escape.

Nobody would catch them now! Shivaji made his way back to the Deccan in disguise, where he was greeted with joy and made King of the Marathas.

Shivaji's exploits, his daring and his good leadership marked the rise of the Maratha kingdom. It was to remain important in Indian history for many years to come.

Plassey

On June 23rd 1757, two armies drew up their battle-lines face to face, outside the village of Plassey, in Bengal. The army of the English East India Company had three thousand men and was commanded by Robert Clive.

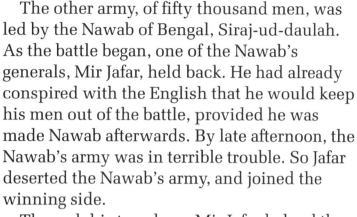

The other army, of fifty thousand men, was led by the Nawab of Bengal, Siraj-ud-daulah. As the battle began, one of the Nawab's generals, Mir Jafar, held back. He had already conspired with the English that he would keep his men out of the battle, provided he was made Nawab afterwards. By late afternoon, the Nawab's army was in terrible trouble. So Jafar deserted the Nawab's army, and joined the winning side.

Through his treachery, Mir Jafar helped the English win the Battle of Plassey. He would become the next Nawab of Bengal and Robert Clive would be remembered for his great victory. After the battle, the English became the real rulers of Bengal. Their conquest of India had begun.

England and France both had trading posts, called factories, in India. Whenever there was a war between the two countries in Europe, there was fighting between the two companies in India. Both countries tried to persuade Indian rulers not to deal with their rivals. Also, whenever Indian states disagreed with each other, France and England took sides. In this way, European powers began to play a part in Indian political affairs.

Clive's victory at Plassey, as well as previous victories in the Carnatic wars in India, meant that the English became strong in India. The Indian rulers were unable to unite, and so couldn't hold them back. In this way, the English changed from being simply merchants and traders in India, to being the rulers of the land.

The tiger of Mysore

Tipu Sultan stood unhappily beneath the great walls of Srirangapatnam. Two of his sons stood beside him, and nearby stood English officers and soldiers. As Governor-General Cornwallis approached, Tipu Sultan pushed his sons gently forward.

The English wanted to hold the two boys as hostages to ensure that Tipu Sultan wouldn't break the peace treaty he had just signed. They hoped that this might destroy Tipu Sultan's power. But they were wrong!

Tipu Sultan was ruler of the southern state of Mysore. When the East India Company took control of Bengal, it also established its headquarters at Madras and Bombay. But when the company tried to take control of Mysore, its ruler, Tipu Sultan, refused to give in. He became the most powerful enemy of the English in India. A brave and fearless fighter, he became known as 'the tiger of Mysore'. He used the tiger as his symbol of power because he admired the beast's ferocity and strength.

Tipu Sultan became well known in India and Europe for his actions. He was the last Indian ruler who had any chance of stopping the British from taking over the whole of the country. He even tried to get support from France, Britain's traditional enemy, to get rid of the intruder.

In 1792, the English sent a great army against Tipu Sultan. The army included sixty-seven elephants and twenty-six thousand bullocks! The army beseiged Srirangapatnam, Tipu's stronghold, for two weeks before he eventually gave in.

The peace treaty that was signed couldn't stop the tiger of Mysore. He continued to fight until 1799, when he died among his soldiers. He was trying once again to defend Srirangapatnam. After Tipu Sultan's death, there was no Indian ruler left who could prevent the British from establishing an empire in India.

Cheap cotton

The chattering women walked across the floor to admire a pile of cotton fabrics lying in the corner of the shop. They stroked the fabrics and admired the patterns printed on them. The fabrics were attractive. They were brightly coloured and well made.

The shopkeeper watched from behind the counter. He had bought the fabrics from an English merchant for a good price and he wanted them to be a success. He felt sorry for the Indian weavers who made fine cloth, but he could make more money by selling these fabrics made in Lancashire, in England.

For centuries, Indian weavers had made bright cotton cloth which they sold at home and in other parts of the world. But in the early 19th century, merchants from Britain began to import cloth made in the mills of northern England. The cloth was good and it was cheap. The merchants made money.

It was more important for the British that their country become rich than that India should prosper. The English merchants soon ruined the trade and livelihood of the Indian weavers. India became nothing more than a supplier of raw materials for British industries, and a market for British manufactured goods, including textiles. Britain needed to control India in order to make sure that its industries were provided with the raw materials they needed.

The people who provided these raw materials in India were badly treated. And the forced growing of crops, like indigo and opium, which provided quick money but neither food nor a stable economy, led to famine. When help was given, it was usually too little and too late. In this way, Britain's political control of India grew.

The great reformer

The two schoolboys climbed the stairs to the second floor of the Bristol Museum and Art Gallery in England. At the top of the stairs, they stopped and looked up at a huge painting in front of them. "Who is it?" asked one of the boys. It was a portrait of Raja Ram Mohan Roy!

Raja Ram Mohan Roy lived in India at the time when the British ruled his country. He was born in a well-to-do brahmin family, and when he was a young man, he went to work for the British at Calcutta. He was very clever and made a lot of money. He was also a scholar who studied philosophy, religion and languages, including Greek, Latin, French, English, Persian, Arabic and Sanskrit.

But Ram Mohan Roy wasn't interested in making money. He really wanted to improve the Indian people's way of life. He knew that some Hindu ideas were very old-fashioned and should be changed. He believed that Indians could learn much from the West, with whom they shared many ideas, without losing their own culture or heritage.

Ram Mohan Roy particularly believed that everyone had the right to be treated with respect. He wanted to see the caste system reformed to prevent one caste from treating another caste badly. He wanted to stop the practice of 'suttee', in which a widow was burned alive on her husband's funeral pyre. And he wanted women to have a higher status and greater respect in the community. Ram Mohan Roy also believed that the English language should be taught in schools, replacing Persian as the official language.

In 1830, Ram Mohan Roy went to Britain where he was able to put forward his ideas. In 1833, he travelled to Bristol. Here, he became ill and died.

Today, Ram Mohan Roy is often called the 'Father of Modern India'. His portrait can be seen in the Bristol Museum and Art Gallery.

Learning from the West

The landowner's son slowly climbed the steps of the government office. He was nervous. His palms were sweating and his legs were shaking. This was his first day at work as a government clerk, and he wanted to make a good impression. If he did well, there would be many years of service ahead of him.

There were many young men like this who learned Western ideas. They were taught in the English language — in fact, it was necessary to know English in order to get a government job. These young men became the first of a new middle class in the cities of India. They usually came from wealthy families. And they learned to think and speak like the British who ruled them. Many Indians could recite more Shakespeare or Byron than most Englishmen!

The new system of education in India was started by Lord Thomas Babington Macaulay. He was an English poet, historian and politician. Macaulay believed that as many young Indians as possible should be persuaded to study Western learning, in the English language. He felt that it was a good thing for the country and its people to be 'civilized' in this way.

Macaulay's system of education produced efficient clerks for the government, but the end of the old system resulted in much illiteracy. However, educated Indians did become aware of the modern thought and civilization of the West.

In 1835, members of the British government decided to spend the money put aside for education in India on English education. Indian culture was no longer recognised as it should have been. Many people felt frustrated at this, in spite of the new ideas and knowledge they had gained.

The Great Revolt

Dark clouds were gathering above the parade ground at Meerut. A storm was approaching. The soldiers stood stiffly to attention, their rifles loaded and ready.

Eighty-five sepoys marched slowly into the middle of the waiting ranks. The sepoys had no guns. When they halted, their army uniforms and boots were torn off and chains were fastened round their ankles. Then they were ordered to march to the prison where they were quickly locked away.

The year was 1857. The sepoys were mutineers. They had refused to load their rifles with a new kind of cartridge when ordered to do so by their officers.

These cartridges had been covered with a greased wrapping as a protection against moisture, which had to be torn open with the teeth before loading. The sepoys believed that the grease was pig and cow fat. As the cow was sacred to the Hindus, and the Muslims were forbidden to touch the pig, they thought that the British were trying to destroy their religion and convert them to Christianity.

On the day after the imprisonment, the storm broke. Those sepoys who hadn't mutinied at Meerut ran through the camp, setting fire to buildings, looting, and killing any European officers they could find. Running to the jail, they released the mutineers. Then they set out for Delhi where they found the last descendant of the Mughals and proclaimed him Emperor of India.

By 1856, Britain ruled about two-thirds of India and had control over the rest. Indians whose kingdoms had been taken were angered by the British. Artisans and craftsmen had been ruined and British rule had made the peasants' life more miserable than ever. There had been many small revolts against the British, but this was the largest.

The Great Revolt only lasted a few months before the British recaptured the cities they had lost. Then, early in 1858, the British soldiers began to take their terrible revenge. Hundreds of mutineers were put to death, and thousands of villages in the north were destroyed. Temples, mosques and palaces were stripped of their treasures. Slowly, the rebellion was crushed and the British re-established their rule over India.

The first railway

"Here comes the train!" Shrieking with delight, the children scrambled up the bank to get a better view. Everyone wanted to catch a glimpse of the new steam-engine.

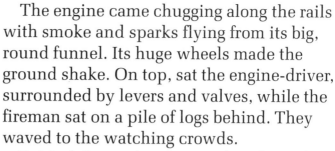

The engine came chugging along the rails with smoke and sparks flying from its big, round funnel. Its huge wheels made the ground shake. On top, sat the engine-driver, surrounded by levers and valves, while the fireman sat on a pile of logs behind. They waved to the watching crowds.

Behind the engine came a long line of carts and wagons loaded with goods, and there was a passenger coach at the back. It was packed with people both inside and out. Some sat on the roof, some hung onto the doors, and dust, smoke and steam swirled around them.

In the 1850s, the railway began operating between Bombay and Thane. The train was pulled by a steam engine. At first, people were unsure about travelling in this way. But they soon got used to it, and even began to enjoy travelling by train.

The first railways were built as an experiment. But within a few years, rails had been laid to nearly all parts of the sub-continent. Trains puffed up the foothills of the Himalayas, along the east coast from Calcutta to Madras, and across the Western Ghats from Bombay to Bangalore.

The railway system was one of the few real benefits to come from British colonial rule at this time, even though it had been built more for the benefit of British traders than for the Indian people. Another was the system of electric telegraph lines which criss-crossed the land, carrying messages over thousands of miles. Life in India was changing rapidly.

Lord Ripon's defeat

The British club house was a cool and shady place. Inside, the men were furious.

"Disgraceful!" muttered one of them, pulling at his long moustache.

"We won't stand for it!" exclaimed another. As he clapped his hands, an Indian servant came hurrying into the club house, carrying a fresh drink.

The year was 1883. Europeans all over India were angry and horrified because of a new law bill called the Ilbert Bill. This had been drawn up by Lord Ripon's law minister. It would allow Indian judges to try Europeans in the courts. Before then, only European judges had been allowed to do this.

The European residents in India simply couldn't believe it. They were used to treating the Indians as inferiors, who could never be equal to Englishmen. It was unthinkable that an Indian should be allowed to sit in judgement on a white person!

The European community gathered together to make their protest heard. They held meetings and signed petitions. They placed angry advertisements in the newspapers attacking the bill. One group even plotted to kidnap Lord Ripon himself!

This storm of protest was so violent that Lord Ripon was forced to give in and the bill was dropped. An Indian judge could still try a European in court, but he must sit with a jury who would decide on the verdict. And at least half the jury members must be European! Of course, this took away any real power from the Indian judges.

The English residents seemed to have won the battle. But their high-handed campaign had upset many Indians. The Indians felt they had been insulted and bullied by the Europeans for over a hundred years. Now they refused to remain second-class citizens in their own country!

The first Congress

"The people of India must have a share in governing their own country!"

Womesh Chandra Bonnerjee finished his speech and sat down. He looked around happily at the other men in the chamber. They were cheering and clapping and waving their papers. It was December 28th 1885, and the first all-Indian political organization had been formed.

The organization, or party, was called the Indian National Congress, and Bonnerjee was its president. This was the first meeting of the party, and it was being held in the city of Bombay.

Seventy-three men from all regions of the country had gathered to discuss the future. They all dreamed of a new India in which Indians enjoyed equal rights, and governed themselves through representatives of the people.

The new Congress party didn't want a revolution. They were mostly upper class, English-educated Hindus, Muslims, Christians and Parsees, who spoke English and had attended college. They were all loyal to the British Crown, but they believed that the British had too much power. They wanted Indians to be admitted to the Civil Service and to other government posts. They were opposed to India's wealth being spent on Britain's wars, and on other affairs not serving Indian interests.

At first, the British rulers welcomed the Indian National Congress. They knew that many people criticized them for taking no notice of the wishes of the Indians themselves. Now they could show that they were ready to take advice from the seventy-three new representatives. The Congress didn't seem to pose a real threat to their colonial rule.

The National Congress continued to meet every year, each time at a different city. The members made many demands for changes in the law, but few of these were met. And when changes were made, they were usually made too late.

Some nationalists grew impatient with this slow progress and they had to leave the organization. Yet, gradually, the Congress grew into a powerful force in India's fight for independence.

The beloved leader

"Freedom is my birthright, and I will have it!"
Bal Gangadhar Tilak had finished his speech.
He looked at the huge, cheering crowd before
him. They had poured into Poona from the
surrounding farms and villages.

The people had come to celebrate the
birthday of the Maratha hero, Shivaji. They
had also come to listen to Tilak, the man they
called Lokamanya, or Beloved Leader of the
People. In 1895, Tilak had revived the Shivaji
festival to remind the Indian people of their
proud history and culture.

Tilak was one of the leaders of the Indian
National Congress. He was a lover of tradition
who wanted India to keep its age-old religious
customs. In 1893, he had revived the birthday
festival for Ganesh, the elephant-headed
Hindu god. He used these festivals to spread
nationalist ideas among the people.

Tilak wanted independence for his country.
He was impatient with the slow reforms
allowed by the British. In his speeches, he
called for 'swaraj', or freedom. He encouraged
his followers to resist the British in many
ways. He encouraged them not to buy British
goods, and to rely on their own strength to win
freedom.

Tilak's campaign had many followers, but in
1907, he was arrested by the British. They tried
him and sent him to prison in Mandalay,
Burma, for six years.

When he returned to India, Tilak was a greater hero than ever before. He rejoined the Congress in 1916 and carried on a campaign demanding self-government for India.

Sadly, Tilak never saw the results of his years of hard work. In 1920, he died, just before a new mass movement was launched by Mahatma Gandhi for India's freedom. That great Indian leader later called Tilak 'The Maker of Modern India'.

Massacre at Amritsar

A huge crowd of people had gathered on a piece of waste ground where they were packed tightly together. A few men had climbed onto a pile of rubble and now began to make speeches. India, they said, must be freed from the British! The time had come for the Indian people to govern themselves! The crowd shouted back in agreement.

This waste ground was called the Jallianwalla Bagh, and it was surrounded by houses. On April 13th 1919, it was packed with thousands of people. Some had come to Amritsar to celebrate a festival. But many more were there to protest against arrests made the day before, and to defy British rule.

Then, outside the Bagh, a line of armoured cars appeared. The people could hear the tramp of army boots. The crowd turned to look. Ninety soldiers were marching up the narrow alley towards them. The soldiers spread out in line and knelt down, pointing their rifles at the huge crowd.

"Don't be alarmed!" shouted one of the speakers. "They will never shoot at us!" But at that moment a command rang out from General Dyer. The soldiers opened fire and for six terrible minutes they fired 1,650 rounds of bullets into the helpless crowd. There were screams of panic as people tried to find a way out of the Bagh.

When the shooting finally stopped, nearly a thousand men, women and children lay dead. Thousands more lay wounded.

News of the massacre quickly spread through the country. At first, the people were deeply shocked by the bloodshed. Then their shock turned to bitterness. They had hoped that the British would hand over power to them peacefully. Now it was clear that the people would have to fight for their independence.

Shantiniketan, House of Peace

The poet strolled beneath the cool shade of the trees. Not far away, he could see a class of boys and girls with their teacher. The teacher was scolding one of the boys, who carried on behaving badly. Suddenly, the teacher lost his temper and smacked him.

The poet was shocked. So he took a slip of paper from his pocket and wrote on it, 'Let me remind you, dear brother, that you cannot turn an ass into a horse by beating it, although you can easily beat a horse into an ass.' That evening, he handed the paper to the teacher. The teacher never smacked a child again.

This poet was called Rabindranath Tagore. In 1901, he had founded a very special school in Bengal, called Shantiniketan, which means 'House of Peace'.

At this school, classes were held in the open air instead of in dreary classrooms. The boys and girls at Shantiniketan learned far more than just reading and writing. They were taught to dance, and to play traditional Indian music. They painted, made pottery and wove baskets and mats. As they spent so much time out of doors, they learned about nature and the changing seasons.

Tagore supervised his school carefully. He made sure that his pupils ate good food. He took many lessons himself and wrote plays for the children to perform. He even wrote new textbooks for them. To pay for the running of Shantiniketan, he sold his house and his books, and his wife sold much of her jewellery.

Tagore's school was only one of the poet's famous achievements. Not only was he a poet, but he was also a writer of plays, short stories and novels, a composer of music, a painter and a well known public figure. He was also a leader in the fight against partition which began in 1905.

Tagore travelled to Europe, America and the Far East, to lecture. He gave the Oxford Lecture on 'Religions of Man'. In 1913, he was awarded the Nobel Prize for Literature and, in 1915, he was knighted by the British. In 1918, he founded the Vishva-Bharati, the World University at Shantiniketan. In 1919, Tagore renounced his knighthood as a protest against the Amritsar massacre.

Rabindranath Tagore

Ramanujan's letter

The oil lamp spread a tiny circle of light, just bright enough for writing by. Srinivasa Ramanujan leaned over the table. He was tired after his day's work, but he must write the letter before he went to sleep. He picked up his pen. 'Dear Sir', he began.

When Ramanujan had finished the letter, he put it in an envelope. He posted the letter the following day. Early in 1913, the letter landed on the desk of Professor Godfrey Hardy, in Cambridge, England. It had travelled thousands of miles.

Hardy was famous in the world of mathematics. He used to study and give lectures at the old university of Cambridge, where he lived in comfortable rooms. He was surprised to receive a letter from a poor and unknown clerk in Madras. But as he read it, his surprise turned to amazement. Ramanujan was clearly a mathematical genius!

Ramanujan had discovered the magic of numbers at the age of fifteen. He had found an old textbook and read through it with great excitement. Soon, he was developing his own ideas. In 1903, Ramanujan won a scholarship to the University of Madras, but afterwards, he found it hard to get a job. He could think of nothing but mathematics and his own new theories.

At last, Ramanujan took a job as a clerk. The job was very badly paid, but Ramanujan managed to carry on with his mathematical work at the same time. In 1911, some of his theories were published in a magazine. Two years later, Ramanujan wrote his letter to Professor Hardy.

This was a turning point in Ramanujan's life. Hardy persuaded him to travel to England. Here, Ramanujan showed himself to be such a brilliant scholar that he was elected to the Royal Society of London, the second Indian to be honoured in this way.

Gandhi's bonfire

"How can we defeat the British? We can stop paying their taxes! We can stop buying their goods!"

The crowd cheered wildly. They craned forward to hear what the speaker would say next. He was a small, stooping man. His head was bald and he wore glasses with wire frames. He was dressed in a white dhoti, or loin cloth, and sandals. His name was Mohandas Karamchand Gandhi.

Gandhi was persuading the people in the crowd to give up all their foreign clothes. They began to collect all garments which were not Indian-made. Shirts, trousers, vests and caps were heaped one on top of the other in a big pile and a bonfire was made of them.

While the fire blazed, Gandhi went on speaking. He begged the people not to buy foreign goods but to spin and weave their own cloth. Gandhi dressed in a dhoti made of homespun cotton, like the poorest Indian. And he used to spend half an hour each day at his little spinning wheel.

Mohandas Karamchand Gandhi had once been a successful lawyer. He had lived in South Africa where he had campaigned against racial discrimination. At first, he had respected the British Empire and its rulers. But the shock of the Amritsar Massacre changed everything. More than ever he wanted independence. He wanted the people to govern themselves without British interference. And he believed that freedom could be gained without riots and bloodshed.

During the year of 1921, Gandhi travelled up and down the land. His message was a simple one. There must be no violence. Instead, the Indian people must stop doing business with the British. That meant paying no taxes and buying no British goods. They must also avoid using British courts and schools. This non-violent policy of resistance was called satyagraha. Gandhi hoped that peaceful rebellion would succeed where fighting had failed.

The great salt march

The tide was out. Gandhi stepped onto the shore and his feet sank into the soft brown mud left behind by the sea. He stooped down to pick up something in his fingers, then he held it up in triumph. It was a lump of salt!

Gandhi had set out from his Ashram in Ahmedabad on March 12th 1930, to walk all the way to Dandi. As usual, he wore only his white homespun dhoti and his sandals, and he carried a long bamboo staff to lean on. The journey took twenty-four days and covered about four hundred kilometres.

Gandhi had started for Dandi with seventy-eight followers. Along the way, he was greeted by hundreds of thousands who lined the route. Some people came on foot, some on bicycles. Some even came in cars. As Gandhi passed, villagers knelt by the side of the dusty road, and women ran out with gifts of food and drink.

Gandhi had made the long journey to the shore simply to pick up salt. He was deliberately disobeying the salt laws. Only the British government was allowed to make and sell salt, and there was also a tax on the sale of salt. Gandhi had encouraged other Indians to follow his example and defy the British.

After Gandhi had picked up his lump of salt, many others did the same. All along the coast, people waded into the water with pans to make their own salt. Hundreds of them were arrested. About a month later, Gandhi himself was arrested and sent to prison.

Newsmen and cameramen sent reports and pictures of the great salt march all over the world. Messages of support flooded in to Gandhi from many different nations. And the march had also set off a huge wave of protest up and down the country.

By the second half of 1930, about 92,000 arrests had been made. Now the people of India knew that, if they acted together, they could challenge the rule of the British.

Bose's escape

"Halt! Who goes there?" The soldier peered into the darkness, his rifle at the ready. His job was to guard the house, and to stop the dangerous rebel, Bose, from escaping. Now, he could see a figure coming out of the shadows. Looking more closely, the soldier saw that it was only an old man. It couldn't possibly be Bose! He relaxed. "That's all right," he said. "Carry on!"

The old man shuffled away and turned a corner. When he was out of sight, he began to run. He reached a waiting car which drove quickly away as soon as its passenger was safely inside. The man relaxed and smiled to himself. He was Subhas Chandra Bose and he had escaped!

The year was 1941 and the Second World War had begun. In Europe, the Germans had invaded Poland and France. In the Far East, the Japanese were about to conquer Singapore and Malaysia, which were at that time British colonies. Bose and his supporters thought this was an ideal time to try and force the British to leave India.

Bose had been arrested because of his activities against the British. And even after he was released, a close watch was kept on his house in Calcutta. After his escape, he made his way to Germany, determined to help in the defeat of the British. He gave daily broadcasts on the radio from Berlin, urging his countrymen to rebel against British rule.

But most Indians didn't want to gain their freedom by seeking the help of Britain's enemies, the Germans or the Japanese.

In 1943, Bose travelled by submarine all the way to Singapore and Tokyo. His aim was to take charge of the Indian National Army, made up of Indian prisoners of war, and enter India from the East and defeat the British. The Japanese welcomed him and soon, Bose had trained an army of thirty thousand people.

Bose and his army set off towards India through Burma. In March 1944, they crossed the border into India. However, after desperate fighting, they were driven back. After Japan had surrendered, Bose escaped in a Japanese plane but was killed when it crashed. His stirring deeds had made him a great nationalist hero.

Freedom at midnight

Jawaharlal Nehru

"At the stroke of the midnight hour, when the world sleeps, India will awake to life and freedom!"

These words were part of Jawaharlal Nehru's speech to the Constituent Assembly, on the night of August 14th 1947. The following day, he was sworn in by Lord Mountbatten as India's Prime Minister. This day, August 15th, became India's Independence Day.

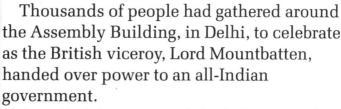

Thousands of people had gathered around the Assembly Building, in Delhi, to celebrate as the British viceroy, Lord Mountbatten, handed over power to an all-Indian government.

As midnight came and the bells chimed, a fanfare of conch shells boomed out. A choir began to sing the patriotic song, 'Vande Mataram'. The cheers grew deafening as the new national flag was unfurled for the first time. At its centre was the wheel of Ashoka.

On August 16th, the new Indian flag was hoisted above the Red Fort at Delhi. Nehru spoke of India's freedom to the people who had gathered in their thousands.

All over India, people celebrated their new freedom. In Mysore, an aircraft flew overhead, showering the people with many-coloured flowers. Political prisoners were released from jail. Sweets were given away to children. In Trivandrum, there was a great rally of bicycles, each one flying the new national flag.

After about two hundred years of colonial rule, the British were leaving India. British civil servants packed up their belongings and left India. Battalions of British soldiers handed over their duties to the new independent Indian army and marched away from the land they had once dominated. The last battalion sailed from Bombay on February 28th 1948. Now, India was free to shape her own destiny.

A divided land

The little boy held on tightly to his father's hand. He was very frightened. The huge, milling crowd jostled all around him, and he was afraid of getting lost. The station was crammed with passengers. They were rushing about, shouting, crying or quarrelling. They carried their belongings in bags and sacks. They had been waiting there for hours.

At last, a train pulled slowly into the station and stopped. It was already packed with passengers. But the people on the platform surged forward, trying to find a place. Everyone was desperate to leave the station.

In August 1947, India became independent. Now it was also a divided land. The British government had agreed to the demands of the Muslim League, an organization that represented a section of India's Muslims. It demanded that a separate state of Pakistan be created. The new state was in north-west India, and in a part of eastern India.

For hundreds of years, Muslims and Hindus had lived peacefully together. But with the division of the country, which was known as partition, panic began. People of the two religions fled from each other in terror. Millions of people were uprooted from their homes. They migrated from India to Pakistan, or from Pakistan to India.

There was dreadful confusion. Roads and railways were blocked with convoys of refugees, some of them stretching for miles! When people of different religions met, they attacked each other. Thousands of people never reached their destinations at all. Trucks were ambushed and burned, and thousands of people were massacred. Many people tried to restore order. Gandhi toured the worst areas of trouble, trying to comfort the people, until he was killed by a Hindu fanatic.

About half a million Hindus, Muslims and Sikhs died during the first months of partition. It was a terrible price to pay for India's freedom.

These musicians, on the banks of the Ganga, are playing on sitar and tabla.

Making music

The musician sits cross-legged. A sitar is cradled against his knee. His left hand begins to move over the strings. At first they go slowly, then faster and faster. On his right forefinger the man wears a pointed plectrum, which he uses for plucking the strings. His left hand moves up and down the fingerboard, bending the strings to make a whining sound.

The haunting music of the Indian sitar is famous throughout the world. The instrument is made of teakwood, and a seasoned gourd, the dried shell of a large fruit. It has seven main strings which are plucked, and thirteen others which provide a musical resonance to the main strings.

The sitar is usually accompanied by two other instruments. The tabla is a set of two small drums, one made of wood and the other of metal. The tanpura is a stringed instrument that keeps the continuity of musical notes with the droning sound. The sarangi, another stringed instrument, is carved from a block of wood. The strings are stretched lengthwide and are played with a bow.

dholak

The shehnai comes from northern India. It is a wind instrument, and is very difficult to play. The shehnai is used at weddings and other joyous occasions.

The bansari is the most popular of all musical instruments. It is made from bamboo and is cheap to carve or to buy. The skills of the bansari flute-players, as with most musical skills, are handed down from father to son. The bansari is a popular folk instrument.

tabla

The jal-tarang is a musical instrument made up of porcelain bowls containing water. Each bowl contains a different amount of water. The number of bowls varies, depending on the tune to be played. When the bowls are struck with sticks, each of them gives out a different note. Sometimes, the jal-tarang player rubs the bowl with wetted fingers instead, to produce a beautiful humming sound.

sarangi

veena

Great sporting moments

The cricket ball soared high into the air. India's captain, Kapil Dev, raced across the turf to catch it. Could he reach it in time? As Kapil Dev caught the ball, cheers went up all round the ground.

The scene was Lord's cricket ground in London, England. The Indian team were playing the West Indies in the final of the 1983 World Cup. It included Sunil Gavaskar, another great cricketer.

The great West Indian team were the favourites to win, but Kapil's great catch changed the course of the match. Soon afterwards, the West Indian batsmen were all out for 140 runs, forty-three runs less than their opponents. India had won the World Cup for the very first time.

Cricket was introduced to India by the British over a century ago. Today, it is one of the most popular of all sports.

Indians have also proved brilliant at hockey, another game introduced by the British. Indian teams won every single hockey tournament at the Olympic Games between 1928 and 1956. Some of the great players became national heroes. Dhyan Chand was one of them.

Indian athletes gained a major sporting triumph at the 1982 Commonwealth Games in Brisbane, Australia. And Indian wrestlers won four gold medals. The most successful was Rajinder Singh, who won the welterweight title for the second time running.

Two sports are especially linked with Indian history. One is the game of chess, which was popular in ancient India and later spread through Persia and Arabia to Europe. The other is polo. Invented in Persia, polo soon had its fans in India, too. Polo has been played on the subcontinent for hundreds of years by Rajput princes, Mughal emperors and British viceroys. Many of the terms used in polo come from Indian words. Each seven-minute period of the game is called a 'chukka', and the riding breeches worn by the players are called 'jodhpurs', after a city in Rajasthan.

The Green Revolution

The farmer looked out over the huge field. Young plants rustled gently in the breeze. So this was the new kind of wheat! The farmer shook his head. It would never be a success. It wouldn't give as big a harvest as the old wheat he had always grown!

The farmer had sown some new wheat seed that year for the first time. The government officer had told him that it had been specially developed by scientists to help him grow more grain. But now this didn't seem possible. The stems on the new crop seemed much too short. They had shot up quickly, and looked as though they would be very weak.

But the farmer was wrong. His harvest that year was larger than ever before. The new wheat grew very quickly and produced two or three times as many grains as the old kind. All over the Punjab and Haryana, the story was the same. Farmers who sowed the new seed were amazed at the results. This was to be the beginning of a Green Revolution in Indian farming.

The Green Revolution started in the 1960s. Agricultural scientists took wheat from Mexico and rice from South-east Asia. By mixing them with native Indian seeds, they managed to produce new varieties which were perfectly suited to the local climate. By the middle of the 1980s, Indian farmers were using these varieties to increase their harvests by more than three times.

Modern tractors are now used instead of bullocks to help plough and do other jobs.

These women in Haryana state are using a machine to thresh wheat.

Besides using new varieties of seeds, Indian farmers began to use new methods of farming. Instead of bullock-drawn ploughs, they used tractors. Instead of manure and compost, they fed the crops with chemical fertilizers. Other new chemicals were sprayed on the fields to prevent pests and diseases. Unfortunately, chemical fertilizers aren't always properly used and, in some cases, terrible damage is done to the soil. Water for irrigation was pumped up from wells deep underground.

The Green Revolution changed Indian agriculture. Today, farmers grow more food than the country needs. The harvest of 1985 was so great that there wasn't enough space in the state warehouses to store the grain. But, despite the revolution, a great number of Indians still live with hunger, low incomes, unemployment, and no land of their own.

A family of tigers drink at a pool.

Project Tiger

The tiger lay snoozing in the heat of the fading sun. Hearing the noise of a bird in the dhak tree, it stirred and looked up. It was nearly time to go hunting!

First, the tiger groomed itself, working its rough tongue all over its fur, starting at the paws. Then it gave a huge yawn and stretched its massive body. Ready at last, it moved off slowly to hunt its evening meal.

This tiger lives in the Ranthambhore Reserve in Rajasthan. There are more than forty tigers in this wildlife sanctuary, as well as hundreds of other species of mammals, reptiles and birds. Here, the tigers are safe from hunters and poachers who might try to shoot them. They live naturally, without being disturbed by people.

The tiger is the most famous and splendid of all Indian animals. Yet, for most of this century, it has been hunted very fiercely.

Tiger-shooting became a popular sport amongst the wealthy and high-born. One Maharajah boasted of having shot more than a thousand tigers by himself. For the tigers, it was nearly a complete disaster. Around the beginning of the 20th century, there were about 40,000 tigers in India. In 1972, a government survey showed that there were only 1,827 tigers left! Within a few years, it seemed, there would be no tigers at all in the sub-continent.

In 1973, the Indian government launched its 'Project Tiger' with the help of the World Wildlife Fund. Nine areas were set aside in Northern India as special reserves. Game wardens were appointed to look after these areas. They were equipped with jeeps, boats, radios and other important items. The race to save the tiger had begun.

Today, India has fifteen 'Project Tiger' reserves and over 240 other wildlife sanctuaries. The tiger population has risen again to more than 4,000. For the moment, at least, this magnificent creature is safe. But its survival remains in our hands.

This picture shows the splendid colouring of the tiger.

Indira Gandhi

"Indira Gandhi ki jai! Long live Indira!"

The milling crowd roared with delight as a frail but sprightly woman in a sari appeared on the lawns of the house.

Indira Gandhi shyly bowed to her gathered supporters and folded her hands in greeting. Cheers echoed all around Parliament House in Delhi. There was the noise of the beating of drums and bugles were blown.

It was January 19th 1966, and Indira Gandhi had been elected Prime Minister. She was the first woman to lead India, and only the second woman Prime Minister in the world. Would she be able to give her country the strong leadership it needed? The crowd was sure she could.

Mrs Gandhi had been born into a powerful and popular family. Her father was Jawaharlal Nehru, who had led the Indian people from the year of Independence, 1947, until his death in 1964.

The young Indira had spent most of her adult life looking after her father. She had accompanied him on foreign journeys, helped him in his election campaigns, and even kept house for him. But she had never wanted to follow in his footsteps. She was a shy person who liked to stay in the background.

Much against her will, Indira was elected as President of the Congress Party in 1959. Then, two years after her father's death, she became India's new leader. "I never wanted to be Prime Minister," she said later. But other Congress politicians persuaded her to accept the post. They believed that she would be easy to control.

Indira soon proved them wrong. She was a strong and clever national leader. Her popularity grew rapidly as she travelled the country, talking to villagers and farmers and visiting the scenes of disasters. In 1971, she won another resounding victory in a general election. Soon, the people of India were calling her 'Mother'.

Mrs Gandhi stayed in office until 1977, when she lost an election for the first time. However, she worked hard to regain the support of the people, and in 1980 became Prime Minister yet again. Now she was in a stronger position than ever before, and one of the most famous and respected leaders in the world. Her long career ended tragically when she was assassinated four years later.

India today

The red rocket sways as it is lifted from the truck. It swings in the air on the end of a huge crane. Many people are standing around. They help to guide the rocket carefully to its place on the launching pad.

The rocket is a small one, as tall as two men. But soon it will be streaking away from the Earth and into the upper atmosphere. Special equipment sits inside its nose cone, which will record details of the flight. These details will help scientists understand weather patterns in the sky.

Many rockets have been launched from the Thumba Rocket Launching Station. This station is located near Trivandrum, in Kerala, and is one of the busiest launching stations in the world. It has drawn the attention of the scientific community of the world. Most of the rockets, together with satellites and rocket fuel, are designed by the scientists of the Indian Space Research Organization.

In 1975, India's first satellite, called Aryabhata, was sent into orbit. Nine years later, the first Indian spaceman, Rakesh Sharma, took off with the crew of the Soviet Soyuz T-II.

Today, India is one of the most important industrial nations in Asia. As well as her ambitious space programme, she has a rapidly growing programme for using nuclear energy. Five power stations in the country use nuclear power to produce electricity. And at Bhabha Atomic Research Centre, near Bombay, scientists are exploring new ways of using nuclear energy.

The electronics industry is also growing fast. Many new computer companies are manufacturing hardware and software to sell in world markets. Micro-chips, conductors and other electronic components are now produced in huge quantities in many parts of India. Indians are determined to be part of the modern, high-tech world in which we live today.

Special words

Aryans   People who moved into north-west India from Central Asia around 2000 BC.

Brahmi   The writings from which most of India's modern scripts come.

brahmin   The priestly class of the varnas — the highest class.

citadel   A walled fortress, usually built on high ground to defend a city.

daina   A kind of drum.

dasyus   The name given to the original inhabitants of India before the Aryans.

Indra   The son of heaven and earth — the warrior god.

jaziyah   A tax that had to be paid by non-Muslims.

jyotisha   A type of astronomy studied by ancient Indians.

kshatriya   The warrior class of the varnas, second to brahmin.

Mahabharata   One of India's two great epic poems. The longest poem ever written.

nadu   A special assembly called from different villages in Chola India.

Prakrit   The language of the common people during Mauryan times.

Ramayana   The second of India's epic poems.

rasa   A mood or emotion, like pain or sorrow, that Indian musicians or dancers must portray in sound or action.

Rig Veda   A collection of hymns written in Sanskrit between 1500 BC and 1000 BC.

sabha	A Brahmin village assembly in Chola India.
Sangam	A festival of poetry and music.
Sanskrit	The Aryan language, which came to be the ancient scholarly Indian.
sepoys	Indian-born members of the British army in India.
Shaka	An era or period of time that began with Kanishka in AD 78.
shudra	The lowest varna of menial servants and labourers.
soma	The energy-giving drink of the gods.
stupa	A great mound built in the Buddha's honour.
Swayamvara	A gathering in which a daughter traditionally chose a husband from a selection of suitors.
ur	A village assembly in Chola India.
varnas	The four groups or classes into which the Aryan people divided themselves.
vaishya	The third varna of artisans, traders and farmers.
vajra	Indra's shining thunderbolt.
Vritra	The demon of drought and famine.
veena	A stringed instrument that looks like a sitar.

Index

This index is an alphabetical list of the important words and topics in this book.

When you are looking for a special piece of information, you can look for the word in the list and it will tell you which pages to look at.

Acknowledgement

The publishers of **Childcraft** gratefully acknowledge the following artists, photographers, agencies and corporations for illustrations used in this volume. All illustrations are the exclusive property of the publishers of **Childcraft** unless names are marked with an asterisk*.

Cover	Donald Harley, B. L. Kearley Limited
6/7	Roy King, Specs Art Agency
8/9	Michael Charlton, B. L. Kearley Limited; Peter Geissler, Specs Art Agency
10/11	Sharon Pallent, Maggie Mundy Artists Agency
12/13	Richard Berridge
14/15	Terry Thomas, Specs Art Agency
16/17	Mrinal Mitra, Maggie Mundy Artists Agency
18/19	Hemesh Alles, Maggie Mundy Artists Agency
20/21	Charles Front
22/23	Trevor Ridley, B. L. Kearley Limited
24/25	Mrinal Mitra, Maggie Mundy Artists Agency
26/27	Mark Peppé, B. L. Kearley Limited
28/29	Richard Berridge
30/31	Sharon Pallent, Maggie Mundy Artists Agency; Robert Harding Picture Library*
32/33	Robert Harding Picture Library*
34/35	Charles Front
36/37	Roy King, Specs Art Agency
38/39	Michael Charlton, B. L. Kearley Limited
40/41	Richard Berridge
42/43	Charles Front
44/45	Robert Harding Picture Library*; Zefa Picture Library (UK) Limited*
46/47	Donald Harley, B. L. Kearley Limited
48/49	Mrinal Mitra, Maggie Mundy Artists Agency
50/51	Mark Peppé, B. L. Kearley Limited
52/53	Charles Front
54/55	Mrinal Mitra, Maggie Mundy Artists
56/57	Roy King, Specs Art Agency
58/59	Robert Harding Picture Library*
60/61	Barry Wilkinson, B. L. Kearley Limited
62/63	Richard Berridge
62/63	Mark Peppé, B. L. Kearley Limited
64/65	Richard Berridge; Robert Harding Picture Library*
66/67	Richard Berridge; M. Holford*; Werner Forman Archive Limited*
68/69	Tony Chance, Specs Art Agency
70/71	Donald Harley, B. L. Kearley Limited
72/73	Mrinal Mitra, Maggie Mundy Artists
74/75	Michael Charlton, B. L. Kearley Limited
76/77	Terry Thomas, Specs Art Agency
78/79	Barry Wilkinson, B. L. Kearley Limited
80/81	Roy King, Specs Art Agency
82/83	Mark Peppé, B. L. Kearley Limited
84/85	Mrinal Mitra, Maggie Mundy Artists Agency; Zefa Picture Library (UK) Limited*
86/87	Donald Harley, B. L. Kearley Limited
88/89	Michael Charlton, B. L. Kearley Limited
90/91	Mark Peppé, B. L. Kearley Limited
92/93	Richard Berridge
94/95	Charles Front
96/97	M. Holford*; Werner Forman Archive Limited*
98/99	M. Holford*; Werner Forman Archive Limited*
100/101	Terry Thomas, Specs Art Agency
102/103	Sharon Pallent, Maggie Mundy Artists Agency
104/105	Mrinal Mitra, Maggie Mundy Artists Agency
106/107	Trevor Ridley, B. L. Kearley Limited
108/109	Charles Front
110/111	Michael Strand, B. L. Kearley Limited
112/113	Richard Berridge
114/115	Mark Peppé, B.L. Kearley Limited
116/117	Roy King, Specs Art Agency
118/119	Trevor Ridley, B. L. Kearley Limited
120/121	Robert Geary, B. L. Kearley Limited
122/123	Trevor Ridley, Specs Art Agency
124/125	Tony Chance, Specs Art Agency
126/127	Robert Geary, B. L. Kearley Limited
128/129	Richard Berridge
130/131	Richard Berridge
132/133	Michael Strand, B. L. Kearley Limited
134/135	Dermot Power, B. L. Kearley Limited
136/137	Trevor Ridley, B. L. Kearley Limited
138/139	Richard Berridge
140/141	Charles Front
142/143	Michael Long; Robert Harding Picture Agency*
144/145	Michael Strand, B. L. Kearley Limited; Allsport*
146/147	Robert Harding Picture Agency*; The Hutchison Library*
148/149	Bruce Coleman Limited*; Zefa Picture Library (UK) Limited*
150/151	Richard Berridge
152/153	Trevor Ridley, B. L. Kearley Limited